POLICY AND PRACTICE IN HE. ....
NUMBER TWENTY-FIVE

Socialising Transgender
Support in transition

POLICY AND PRACTICE IN HEALTH AND SOCIAL CARE

See www.dunedinacademicpress.co.uk for details of all our publications

POLICY AND PRACTICE IN HEALTH AND SOCIAL CARE

SERIES EDITORS

CHARLOTTE L. CLARKE AND CHARLOTTE PEARSON

Socialising Transgender
Support in transition

Kate Norman

Visiting Fellow at the School of Health in Social Science,
University of Edinburgh

EDINBURGH ◆ LONDON

First published in 2017 by Dunedin Academic Press Ltd.
Head Office: Hudson House, 8 Albany Street, Edinburgh EH1 3QB
London Office: 352 Cromwell Tower, Barbican, London EC2Y 8NB

ISBNs:
9781780460659 (Paperback)
9781780465715 (ePub)
9781780465722 (Kindle)

British Library Cataloguing in Publication Data
A catalogue record for this book is available from the British Library

Typeset by Makar Publishing Production, Edinburgh
Printed in Great Britain by CPI Antony Rowe

CONTENTS

ACKNOWLEDGEMENTS

I am grateful for the financial support of the Economic and Social Research Council (ERSC) and the Scottish government, which supported me during three of the five years of the PhD research underpinning this book. I benefited greatly from the thoughtful supervisory support of Lynn Jamieson and Charlotte Clarke, and, in the first year of the PhD particularly, from Liz Bondi too. My examiners, Raewyn Connell and Heather Wilkinson, provided both valuable and detailed feedback on the thesis.

The research was aided by the support and cooperation of the Scottish Transgender Alliance which gave feedback on draft versions of the questionnaires, and which facilitated their circulation to transgender people and transgender organisations across Scotland. Particular thanks are due to James Morton and Nathan Gale for their assistance in these matters. I must also acknowledge the support of the members of Tyne Trans who assisted in the pilot study, which preceded my research in Scotland. I was also assisted by Lesley Horne who facilitated the circulation of the questionnaire to each Scottish local authority via the Association of Directors of Social Work (ADSW) Contracts Officers Group, and who, together with Andrea Beavon, gave valuable feedback on the draft version of this questionnaire.

I am very grateful to the forty-seven transgender people who completed survey one, to the twenty-seven transgender people who completed survey two, and to the twenty people who completed survey three on behalf of statutory and voluntary agencies. I am also deeply grateful to the nine people from the statutory and voluntary agencies and to the ten transgender people who took part in online interviews. Each of these contributors often offered very personal and thoughtful insights which enhanced the research findings considerably.

I am indebted to my editor, Charlotte Clarke, who has been a source of positive and thoughtful support over the year that I have spent writing, since her initial suggestion for the book. Many aspects of it have been discussed and considered with her, via email and in person, and her kind and prompt responses to my queries and ideas have enabled me to maintain both momentum and positivity in my writing. I have also appreciated her conscientious liaison with myself and Anthony Kinahan at Dunedin Academic Press, who has also provided helpful advice and support.

Lastly I have been very appreciative of the support of my son Daniel, who diligently proof-read the research findings chapters of the thesis and several draft chapters of this book. He has offered many useful suggestions for improvement, and has been willing to discuss, consider and often to offer an alternative perspective to my ideas, conjectures and writings, as they developed over time.

INTRODUCTION

The main purpose of this book is to summarise recent research into the social care of transgender people in a readily accessible form, while highlighting social care needs alongside those for medical care. Recent research through online surveys and interviews by the author into the social care needs and support of transgender people in Scotland (Norman, 2015a, hereinafter referred to as the 'Scottish 2015 study' is juxtaposed with additional research and writings on key transgender issues.

The media attention currently granted to transgender people is usually welcome, but perhaps has too often exposed the discomfort that society experiences in relation to those who do not conform to gender norms – the need to recognise and respond to the social dilemmas raised by such non-conformity is a thread that runs throughout these eight chapters.

The book is written with a broad spectrum of potential readers in mind:

Academics in gender studies may be interested in how the growing body of research into transgender matters affects our understanding of gender. Of particular relevance may be the gender identities and experiences of non-binary transgender people, as well as those who transition to the opposite binary role (Chapters 1 and 3), and how society responds to such migration (Chapters 4, 7 and 8).

Those who currently provide support to transgender people (most notably gender identity clinic staff, GPs, psychiatrists and counsellors, transgender support groups, health workers and social carers) may find the evaluation of potential social care support to transgender people and their families of particular relevance. This evaluation is one of the main underlying themes of the book (Chapters 1–7).

Families, friends, colleagues and neighbours may welcome the material relating to partners and children of transgender people, other family members and those who share their work spaces and neighbourhoods (Chapters 6 and 7). They may also find that the broader perspective that the book offers may assist in gaining a better understanding of the needs of a transgender person (for example, within Chapters 1 and 3–5).

Transgender people themselves may be particularly interested in the research into the types of social support that may be of assistance to them at different stages of their lives (Chapters 1–7).

The book concludes by promoting a greater understanding and acceptance of transgender people, a wider provision of dedicated social care support to augment current medical service provision, and advocacy for the recognition of a 'transgender' legal status in addition to that of 'male' or 'female'.

GLOSSARY OF TERMS

These necessarily simplified working definitions are based on reference to a range of texts.

Bi-gender, a-gender, poly-gender, fuzzy gender, androgyne, gender queer, gender outlaw etc.
Terms used to describe a wide range of people whose self-perception of their gender identity does not conform to the binary gender norm and who may adjust their gendered behaviour accordingly.

Biological sex
The state of biological variables that can be described as either male-typical, female-typical or intersex, (e.g. genetic material, gonads, internal and external genital structures, hormonal profiles).

Cis-gendered
A person who identifies with the sex and gender to which they were assigned at birth.

Cross-dresser
A person who dresses in the clothing of the opposite gender for personal pleasure, usually without the intention of permanent migration to that role.

FtM, Trans-man, Trans-male, Transgender male/man, Transsexual male/man, etc.
Terms used to describe a transsexual person who is migrating or has migrated from their original female gender role to live permanently in a male gender role.

GIC
Gender Identity Clinic

Gender
The state of being male, female or transgender, either self-perceived or perceived by others.

Gender dysphoria
A condition where there is a marked difference between a person's expressed and/or experienced gender, and the gender others would assign to them, continuing for at

least six months, causing clinically significant distress, and/or impairment in social, occupational or other important aspects of life.

Gender identity
The sense or self-perception of belonging to either the binary male or female gender categories, or to a transgender category.

Gender reassignment/confirmation
The transition process by which a transsexual person confirms their internal sense of gender identity, through the external reassignment of their bodily characteristics and gender role, often with the assistance of hormonal and/or surgical intervention.

Gender role
A short-hand term for a blend of forms of self-expression (e.g. mannerisms, styles of dress, activities) that usually convey to oneself and others one's membership of a binary gender or transgender category. Such a multiplicity of forms of expression may fall within a wide range of binary masculine or feminine stereotypical behaviours within society, but, within a transgender role, may be combined in unusual, non-binary ways.

Intersex
A person whose development and differentiation of sex characteristics in utero is atypical, and who was born, for example, with a blend of both male and female internal and/or external genitalia.

LGBT
A shorthand way of referring to lesbian, gay, bisexual and transgender people as a group. This may sometimes be further extended: for example, LGBTQI (lesbian, gay, bisexual, transgender, queer (or questioning) and intersex).

MtF, Trans-woman, Trans-female, Transgender female/woman, Transsexual female/woman, etc.
Terms used to describe a transsexual person who is migrating or has migrated from their original male gender role to live permanently in a female gender role.

Migrator
A subdivision of transgender: a person, more commonly known as transsexual, who seeks to live permanently in the opposite binary gender role to that in which they were initially raised.

Oscillator
A subdivision of transgender: a person who undertakes cross-dressing but for whom this always implies the intention to return to their original gender (*see* Cross-dresser).

Real-life test/experience
A required period (usually one year) during which a transsexual lives full-time in their preferred gender role usually prior to an application for gender reassignment/confirmation surgery.

Scottish 2015 Study
A sequence of research carried out by the author which included a pilot questionnaire and focus group, three online surveys, and nineteen online interviews of transgender people and providers and/or commissioners of dedicated and/or generic social care support to transgender people across Scotland (see Norman, 2015a, and also the Appendix to this book for more details).

Sexuality
A person's sexual orientation or preference.

Social care
The provision of paid or voluntary support necessary for the advocacy, welfare, maintenance and protection of someone, by a family member, friend, neighbour or colleague or by a group or organisation within the community, informally or linked with a formally assessed need.

SDS
Self-directed support

SRS
Sex reassignment surgery

STA
Scottish Transgender Alliance

Transcender
A subdivision of transgender that accommodates people who seek to live outwith binary gender categories.

Transgender
A person whose self-identity does not correspond to the gender linked with their biological sex and/or their initial gender role, or who experiences dysphoria in conforming to conventional notions of a male or female binary gender role.

Transphobia
Dislike of or prejudice against transgender or transsexual people, which may be expressed through subtle forms of discrimination but may also be apparent through more overt acts of rejection including verbal and physical abuse.

Transsexual

A transgender person who wishes to or who seeks to resolve their gender dysphoria through gender reassignment/confirmation, in order to live permanently in the opposite binary gender role.

Transvestite

See the term Cross-dresser, which is increasingly preferred as a descriptive by those who undertake oscillating gender behaviours.

LIST OF TABLES

CHAPTER 1

Gender and Transgender Identities

Introduction

At the turn of the twenty-first century, the term transgender still lacked a universal meaning outwith the world of transgender (and lesbian, gay, bisexual and intersex) people, and the boundaries of direct service providers, policymakers and academia. Public and media interest in those who sought gender reassignment/confirmation in the previous fifty years had, however, been significant, fuelled by the publicity surrounding Christine Jorgenson in 1952 in the USA ('the most famous transgender person in the world', Stryker, 2008, p. 48), and accorded to Roberta Cowell in the UK two years earlier. Cowell may be one of the earliest transgender people to acknowledge the importance of the construction of gender roles: 'I always had to remember that I was building a new personality' (Hausmann, in Stryker and Whittle, 2006, p. 343).

The growth in social awareness of transgender

Meyerowitz notes that 'by the mid-1950s the mass media were reporting constantly on sex change' (Meyerowitz, 2002, p. 97). This seemingly insatiate interest continued with the serialisation of Jan Morris' (1974) autobiography *Conundrum* in the *Sunday Times*. Public exposés in the tabloid press, and critical feminist perspectives within the broadsheet press and in some academic publications, ensured that the topic remained consistently newsworthy.

The initial emphasis on printed media gradually moved to television, with, for example, the inclusion of a trans-woman in *Coronation Street* (albeit played by a non-trans actor) from 1998 to 2014, a trans-woman played by a trans-woman (Laverne Cox) in *Orange is the New Black* from 2013 and the widespread success of the Amazon series *Transparent* from 2014. This was supplemented with an increasingly common 'reality or docu-drama' approach to the lives of transgender people on television, including the ground-breaking series *My Transsexual Summer* (Channel Four, 2011). Such milestones can be credited with bringing a breadth of transgender issues to a wide audience, and, importantly, helped to move the focus away from surgical transformation, for as Cox herself suggested 'the preoccupation with transition and surgery objectifies trans people. And then we don't get to really deal with the real lived experiences' (Cox, 2014).

This chapter begins the process, which continues throughout this book, of clarifying the degree to which recent academic research has aided our understanding of transgender 'real lived experiences', by exploring what is understood by the terms gender, sex and, of course, transgender.

Gender and gender roles

With increasing recognition that gender and gender roles are inextricably linked, it seems unreasonable – if not impossible – to consider one without the other. Byne, for example, explains that gender refers to 'factors related to living in the social role of a man or woman' while adding that gender also refers to the *social categories* of man or woman, boy or girl (Byne, 2007, pp. 65–6, italic added) indicating that gender is not simply self-perceived: it is a label attached to us (which may cause us to modify our behaviour accordingly) by those with whom we interact or who observe us. Twenty years earlier, West and Zimmerman developed the concept of 'doing gender' which, they argued, creates 'differences between girls and boys and women and men, differences that are not natural, essential or biological'. They suggested that once differences have been constructed they are used to reinforce the 'essentialness' of gender (West and Zimmerman, 1987, pp. 131–7).

The concept of social control formed an essential part of Herdt's reflection on Rubin's (1975) view that exaggeration of sex differences suppresses equality between the sexes, creating 'a taboo against the sameness of men and women, (so) dividing the sexes into two mutually exclusive categories (and) thereby *creates* gender' (Herdt, 1996, p. 55, italic original). More recently, Connell notes the 'careful critique' by Pringle (1992) which raised the concern that 'the masculine was consistently more highly valued' (than the feminine) (Connell, 2009, p. 58) while Bradley argues that 'the usage of the term (gender) has been persistently bound up with power relations between women and men' (Bradley, 2007, p. 4), reflecting Millett, Mitchell and Rubin's linking of 'the concept of gender to a theory of inequality and oppression of women' in the early 1970s (Bradley, 2007, p. 16).

Notions of gender power, status and inequality are deeply relevant to an understanding of transgender, for the transition of transsexual people is likely to have a significant effect on their status with others. It may, however, be difficult to clearly distinguish whether such a change in status is consequential on increased visibility as a transgender person, or is linked with the status of the adopted alternate binary role. For example, a MtF transitioned person may find their status reduced or questioned if they are perceived as a transgender person within bi-gendered and women's spaces, or they may find that, if they are accepted as a woman, the status they held when living as a man has suffered as a consequence of transition. Conversely, a FtM person may find that, as their transgender visibility decreases, their status as a male increases: Fine (2010, p. 54) notes the experience of Ben Barres, a professor of neurobiology at Stanford University, and a FtM transsexual, who recalled that 'shortly after I changed sex, a faculty member was heard to say "Ben Barres gave a great seminar today, but then his work is much better than his sister's" ' (Barres, 2006, p. 134).

Unusually within much contemporary writing on gender, Byne distinguishes between 'gender identity' as 'one's sense of belonging to the male or female gender category', and 'gender role' which refers to 'behaviours (e.g. mannerisms, style of dress, activities) that convey to others one's membership in one of these categories' (Byne, 2007, p. 66). This contrasts with academic theory that gender identity is a consequence of repeated performance within prescribed gendered patterns of behaviour. Such a distinction is very relevant to the subject matter of this book because many transgender narratives make just such a distinction, often noting an early awareness of a conflict between inner gender identity and outer gender role.

That interactions with others form an essential element of gender is stressed by Connell when she argues that 'gender is, above all, a matter of the social relations within which individuals and groups act', concluding that 'gender is the structure of social relations that bring reproductive distinctions between bodies into social processes' (Connell,

2009, pp. 10–11). Bradley expands this link with the rituals of courtship and reproductive behaviour to include 'the sexual divisions of labour and cultural definitions of femininity and masculinity' (Bradley, 1996, p. 205). She describes 'the process of doing gender as *gendering*' (Bradley, 2007, p. 23, italics original), reflecting Butler's argument that the 'acts, gestures, enactments (of gendered behaviour) are *performative* in the sense that the essence or identity that they otherwise purport to express are *fabrications* manufactured and sustained through corporeal signs and other discursive means' (Butler, 1990, p. 185, italics original). Hence, to Butler, gender is not a performance representing an inner sense of being but performance is the essence of gender itself.

Both Connell (2009, p. 5) and Butler (1990, p. 11) quote de Beauvoir's famous comment that 'one is not born but rather becomes a woman' (de Beauvoir, 1949, reprint 1997, p. 295), evidencing de Beauvoir's apparent affirmation of the social construction of gender. Bradley paraphrases and expands this statement to argue that 'one is born with a body that is immediately ascribed a male or female identity (usually on the basis of fairly unambiguous physiological evidence, the possession of a penis or a vagina) but one becomes a man or a woman through social interactions within a set of cultural understandings of femininity and masculinity' (Bradley, 2007, p. 21). The expectation that men and women possess male or female bodies underpins West and Zimmerman's distinction between 'sex' and 'sex category', the latter being based on 'the *presumption* that essential criteria exist and would or should be there if looked for' (West and Zimmerman, 1987, p. 132, italic original). This concept may aid the passing of those transgender people who are not 'read', but may not do so for transgender persons who have undertaken transitioning but who do not pass well, whose essential criteria may be subsequently questioned or presumed to be contradictory to their adopted sex category.

The social construction of gender on an individual level might also be extended to gender in groups, and to gender geographies, where social practices and spaces are denoted as male and female, criteria that may exclude a transgender presence. Although Browne *et al.* have questioned 'geography's presumption of man/woman and male/female' (Browne *et al.*, 2010, p. 573), Formby's exploration of 'LGBT communities in the twenty-first century' suggests that '*space*' forms an important part of understandings and experiences of such communities, leading to meeting places for LGBT people within safe locations (some of which may also be open to the public) where additional commonalities of *shared experience* related to identity ... facing prejudice or discrimination ... and (to a lesser extent) *politics*' could be explored (Formby, 2012, p. 65, italics added).

Sex and intersex

Although the notion of sex has not been subject to the widespread level of critical discussion that gender has received, Whittle and Turner cite the biologist Fausto-Sterling (1992) who, they note, has 'argued mischievously that, with manifest variations of chromosomal configurations, there were five sexes rather than two' and go on to question the sex/gender distinction, recognising that it has been much debated and still 'remains contested' (Whittle and Turner, 2007, pp. 3, 5).

Harper, referring to critiques of the treatment of people born intersex by Kessler (1990) and Dreger (1998), proposes that 'the simple dichotomies of sex and gender, and the essentialisms of biological determinism, are destabilised within a biology increasingly understood as medically invented' (Harper, 2007, p. 7). A decade earlier, Diamond and Sigmundson had laid the basis for practitioners within the field of intersex, with guidelines reflecting a changing perspective of persons with ambiguous genitalia (Diamond and Sigmundson, 1997b), following a 'long-term follow up to a classic case' who had been initially raised as a girl but who 'was later found to reject the sex of rearing' (Diamond and Sigmundson, 1997a, p. 298). Meadow suggests that practices that rely on the determination of clear-cut sex differences 'maintain the illusion of dichotomous gender while at the same time (they) demonstrate the larger social purpose that these categories serve' (Meadow, 2010, p. 831).

There are similarities between the destabilisation of sex and gender through the treatment of people born intersex (which in many cases has involved gender assignment shortly after birth, usually based on the appearance of the genitals) and the blurring of legal criteria of sex and gender resulting from the treatment of transgender people. At about the same time as Harper's observations, Whittle and Turner suggested that 'legal sex has never been consistently determined by biology' and that 'normatively in the sex gender distinction, sex precedes gender' whereas within the UK Gender Recognition Act 2004 'one's gender precedes one's sex. One's acquired *gender* becomes the *sex* in which one is recognised in law' (Whittle and Turner, 2007, pp. 16–18, italics original; United Kingdom Government, 2004). A transgender person in the UK, on receiving a Gender Recognition Certificate (GRC), is legally confirmed as their 'new' gender, while their sex also now matches this gender, backdated, if desired, to their date of birth. The binary norm is thus stringently reinforced for transgender people by the 2004 Act regarding gender and sex categories, a conformity that those who feel that they fit within both the binary gender and sex of their migratory role may find reinforcing but which those who do not feel that they fit within either category may find restrictive for essentially misrepresenting their sense of reality as a transgender person.

Binary and transgender identities

More than forty years ago, the psychologists Maccoby and Jacklin (1974) suggested that cognitive theories of 'self-socialisation', by which a child copies certain behaviours because they are old enough to understand that this is normalised behaviour for a child of their own gender, appear to play an increasingly important part after a child's gender identity has been established. Their suggestion that the establishment of gender identity pre-empts the effectiveness of performative routines contrasts with Butler's concept of gender and gender identity as reiterated social performance. Such a perspective of gender, extending beyond that of simply performance or role, is reinforced by Richardson who suggests that it is through a range of learning processes, 'for example observation, imitation, modelling, differential reinforcement (and) agencies of socialization (for example, parents, teachers, peers, the media)' that children learn 'the social meanings, values, norms and expectations associated with "being a girl" or "being a boy"' (Richardson, 2008, p. 9).

Psychological research has long suggested that one's sense of self as a boy or girl usually develops early in childhood, although Smith and Cowie note that 'the results of research in the infancy period (up to two years) do not reveal many consistent behavioural differences between boys and girls. The similarities certainly outweigh the dissimilarities' (Smith and Cowie, 1991, p. 145). However, they note, in the intervening years to school age, that stronger preferences for same-sex playmates and gender stereotypical activities become apparent. What is stereotypical across cultures, and across generations within a culture, will change and develop, but whether it is the *a priori* development of gender identity that leads to apparent gender differences of behaviour, or whether 'being assigned to a specific gender provides a set of ground rules that govern our behaviour, establishing a cornerstone of identity' (Woodward, 2008, p. 83), still appears to be a basic issue of contention which underpins many of the ongoing discussions about the nature of gender and gender identity.

One aspect of our understanding of gender identity that has developed from the notion of self-socialisation is the notion of the importance of active response to agencies of socialisation of gender roles. Connell, for example, stresses the active nature of gender learning, 'the *pleasure* which is obvious (and the) enthusiasm with which young people take up gender symbolism' (Connell, 2009, pp. 95–7, italic original). A contemporary reflexive, reactive model of social learning is, therefore, hypothesised to replace a deterministic model of 'totally passive and totally malleable' infants and children, which has understandably been rejected (Stanley and Wise, 2002, p. 272). Davies, for example, illustrates the active 'location' that children undertake on either side of the gender binary as they construct their own understanding of being boys or girls when she describes how:

> I once gave a toy car to a three-year old girl as a symbolic refusal of the gender order. She unwrapped the present, looked at my (*sic*) quizzically and said, 'It's really a boy's toy, but don't worry, I can handle it', at one and the same time reconstituting the gender order that I was attempting to break down, and taking care, as girls should, not to hurt my feelings too much at having my error pointed out to me (Davies, 2002, p. 281).

Incidentally, this anecdote perhaps offers a useful example of 'female empathizing' behaviour, which, Baron-Cohen argues, contrasts with 'male systemizing' behaviour. He argues that such a distinction *on average* supports the notion of gender-related differences in male and female psychological profiles (with overlapping between the two) (Baron-Cohen, 2003, p. 183). He links these different behaviour patterns to levels of prenatal testosterone, between eight and twenty-four weeks into pregnancy, rather than to processes of socialisation (Baron-Cohen, 2003, pp. 98–111).

Social processes are likely to be contributory too, for as Bradley suggests:

> ...while some of the old insights from socialization are useful in showing where ideas of normality come from and in revealing the pressures we are under as individuals to be 'normal', the more active idea of gendering allows us to explore how individuals develop as agents in interaction with their environment (Bradley, 2007, pp. 23–4).

Such an interactive approach to how individuals develop a gendered niche may also be reflected outwith the binary, through the blending of a multiplicity of gendered forms of self-expression, conveying to oneself and to others both a sense of individuality and of membership within a transgender identity.

Meanwhile, to return to psychological research into the development of gender identity, researchers have also linked this with concepts of gender stability and gender constancy. Smith and Cowie, for example, indicate that gender identity, once initially established, leads boys and girls to the realisation that they will grow up to be men and women (the concept of gender stability) and that this principle applies to other boys and girls too, by about the age of four or five (Smith and Cowie, 1991, p. 146). It had been thought that the realisation that it is not possible for a boy to simply change and become a girl, for example by growing their hair long, or for a girl to become a boy by wearing boys' clothes (gender constancy) developed at about the age of seven years of age (or earlier if the child understood the differences between male and female genitals (Bern, 1975). However, Intons-Peterson's more recent study suggests that children may actually be aware of gender constancy as young as three years and nine months (Intons-Peterson, 1988, as discussed by Kennedy and Hellen, 2010).

Kennedy and Hellen go on to note Kessler and McKenna's finding (Kessler and McKenna, 1978, p. 102) 'that children start to understand gender identity between ages 3 and 4, and that this develops over the next two years as they also become aware of social interpretations of gender as an "invariant" category' (Kennedy and Hellen, 2010, p. 28). It seems that this may also be the stage at which transgender children recognise their difference. Whittle suggests that 'transsexual people will, without exception, say that they have always known that something was wrong' (Whittle, 2000, p. 19). It is, therefore, not unusual (though apparently not 'without exception' – see Connell, 2010) to come across transgender people's early recollections of the discord of being transgender:

> I was three or perhaps four years old when I realized that I had been born into the wrong body, and should really be a girl. I remember the moment well, and it is the earliest memory of my life (Morris, 1974, p. 11).

Kennedy and Hellen's online study of 121 respondents from transgender forums in the UK identified a modal average of five years and a mean average of 7.9 years for the age at which transgender people remembered feeling that their gender identity was at variance with their gender role assigned at birth (Kennedy and Hellen, 2010, p. 28). Such a distinction by transgender people between gender role and gender identity highlights the question of whether it is a binary or transgender person's sense of self as 'boy' or 'girl', 'man' or 'woman' that fluctuates according to the degree of their gender conformity, as a literal reading of Butler's notion of performativity might imply, or whether what fluctuates is the degree to which they identify with masculine or feminine behavioural traits and, in the case of transgender people, experience dissonance between such behaviours and their gender identity.

The potential importance of psychological research into the formation of gender identity is reflected in Billings and Urban's recognition that 'although some physicians asserted that biological predispositions for transsexualism might yet be discovered, most stressed early socialisation in their etiological accounts' (Billings and Urban, 1996, p. 104). This emphasis on the role of early cross-gender socialisation faces similar uncertainties/conflicts between the role of *a priori* development of transgender identity leading to apparent reinforcement of cross-gender behaviours by a sympathetic adult figure, or the contrasting possibility of early parental treatment, inappropriate to societal gender norms, establishing a cornerstone of transgender identity which is then impervious to socialisation within the gender role appropriate to the child's sex. Recent developments in equal gender treatment of pre-school children may raise concern in such a context (see, for example, the discussion of kindergarten-aged boys being persuaded by teachers to dress in skirts by Hoff Sommers, 2013, p. 66).

Such an emphasis on environmental or sociological factors (rein-forced by research in the 1960s and 1970s – see, for example, Money and Tucker, 1976, p. 91) has been balanced by increasing research into the role of biological factors. Benjamin (1966) first speculated on a potential link between oestrogen levels in the womb and transsexuality in the male, and on a link between an abnormal conversion of oestrogen into testosterone in the womb and transsexuality in the female. Twenty years later, Jacklin noted that, 'in research on how hormones affect behaviour and how behaviour affects hormones, the empirical data col-lection necessary to answer basic questions about sex differences has only just begun' (Jacklin, 1989, pp. 129, 131), although Hoff Sommers draws attention to the research of Kimura (1999), which explored the role of hormones in children's gendered play choices, counterbalancing socialisation theories (Hoff Sommers, 2013, p. 67) (see also Baron-Cohen's research into the link between prenatal hormones and empa-thising/systemising behaviour referred to above). Research involving post-mortems of transsexuals' brains (Zhou *et al.*, 1995), and recent genetic evidence indicating that MtF transgender people may have genetic abnormalities linked to 'repeat length polymorphisms in the androgen receptor' (Hare *et al.*, 2009, p. 93), add support to the argu-ment that there is perhaps a biological basis for transgender identities.

Money (1994), who for many years advocated an environmental aetiology for transgender identity, came to believe that multifacto-rial biological and environmental influences are more likely, and this view continues to be endorsed, for example within Byne's discussion of endocrine influences linked with the developing brain's sensitiv-ity to androgen and testosterone secretions *in utero*, for he concludes that 'cognitive and experiential factors must also be considered' (Byne, 2006, p. 956). Such a point of view is taken within the recent House of Commons Report on Transgender Equality, which notes com-ments from the Tavistock Clinic that 'gender non-conformity cannot be explained adequately within any monolithic theoretical model and that explanations are probably multi-factorial' (House of Commons Women's and Equalities Committee, 2016, p. 50).

Kennedy and Hellen note the 'tension between societal expectations of gendered behaviour and ... people (who) are unable to conform to gender norms' (Kennedy and Hellen, 2010, p. 38), referring to transgender people's restricted ability to express what they may perceive as their 'real' gender identity to others, at least widely. Hellen suggests that this may lead to the early internalisation of transphobia, commenting that 'as transgendered children become more aware of how socially unacceptable they may be, the more likely it will be that, rightly or wrongly, they will suppress or at least conceal their gender identities' (Hellen, 2009, p. 84). Kennedy and Hellen suggest that consequential secretive cross-dressing and non-conformist gender expression appear to be 'one of the main common experiences of MtF transgender children' (Kennedy and Hellen, 2010, p. 38). They query Butler's (1993, p. 232) argument that 'femininity is not a choice but the forcible citation of a norm, one whose complex historicity is indissociable from relations of discipline, regulation, punishment', because, they argue, 'although transgender children are subjected to considerable and sustained pressure to conform to gender roles assigned at birth ... in defiance of this they still develop a transgender identity' (Kennedy and Hellen, 2010, p. 39).

From the transgender child's perspective, their sustained sense of difference and isolation, carried throughout childhood and adolescence into adulthood, underpins a conflict between internal gender identity and internalised expectations of appropriate gendered behaviour on a daily basis. Transgender people have mainly come into the public eye in the last sixty years through adult narratives of transition, but the developmental perspectives and dilemmas of transgender children are also gradually achieving comparable widespread recognition and understanding (as, for example, in the programme *Kids on the Edge: The Gender Clinic* (Channel Four, 2016). Empathy for such children also needs to recognise the dilemmas that their parents face, particularly as puberty becomes imminent. Adams recently reported on an interview with the head of the Tavistock Clinic, who cautioned that to think of gender dysphoria only as something to be fixed by hormone treatment is really a 'medicalisation of the complexities of identity and once you have done that you look only for medical solutions'. He notes that 'the Tavistock is soon to begin publishing its own research into a … group of children who have been given hormone block-ers (since) 2011' (Adams, 2016).

Support with gender identity issues

From the Scottish 2015 study of transgender people in Scotland, Table 1.1 summarises the importance of eleven sources of advice or support in helping to come to terms with gender identity. Transgender groups were rated as the most highly valued source of support by over a third (seventeen of forty-seven) of respondents although it was noted that not all respondents had access to such support groups. In addition, further cross-tabulation of the data indicated that transgender groups were considered less likely to meet their needs by MtF rather than FtM individuals although the reason for this is unclear (Norman, 2015a, pp. 221–8).

While more than a quarter (thirteen) of respondents rated gender specialists at a GIC as a very highly valued source of support for gender identity issues, nine respondents considered them to be the least valued source of support. There was little difference in the way that FtM or MtF respondents perceived this source of support.

Eight of the ten respondents in a current male gender role and with a male gender identity placed family members in the three highest categories for support with gender identity issues (with just one of these respondents rating family members in the three lowest categories for such support). Conversely, of the sixteen respondents in a current female gender role and with a female gender identity just six placed family members in the three highest categories, with seven respondents rating them in the three lowest categories. These findings reinforce Whittle et al.'s evidence of lower levels of family support to MtF transgender people than to those who are FtM (Whittle et al., 2007, p. 69).

Similarly, five of the ten respondents in a current male gender role and with a male gender identity rated close friends in the three highest catego-ries for support with gender identity issues (with just one of these respond-ents rating close friends in the three lowest categories for such support). Conversely, of the fifteen respondents in a current female gender role and with a female gender identity only six placed close friends in the three high-est categories for support with gender identity issues, with five respondents rating them in the three lowest categories.

Gender and Transgender Identities   13

Table 1.1: The importance of sources of advice or support in helping come to terms with gender identity (Survey one: n = 47: 47 respondents).

Key: Importance of sources of advice and support regarding gender identity (1 = highest importance, 11 = least importance).

Source/Importance of advice or support in helping come to terms with gender identity	1	2	3	4	5	6	7	8	9	10	11
a. Close friends	13	9	2	4	3	2	1	0	0	1	10
b. Family members	10	7	8	2	3	2	0	3	1	1	9
c. Colleagues at work/line manager	4	3	2	1	2	4	0	3	2	5	15
d. Transgender support group	17	5	3	4	4	2	1	1	1	2	3
e. General practitioner	5	3	8	3	6	5	2	0	3	1	9
f. Gender specialist at GIC	13	1	6	2	4	3	1	2	1	3	9
g. Speech therapist	6	1	1	1	1	5	2	3	3	1	17
h. Health visitor or district nurse	0	0	1	1	1	3	4	1	2	2	25
i. Counsellor or psychiatrist	10	2	6	4	3	1	3	4	0	3	9
j. Social worker	1	0	0	1	0	2	3	2	2	4	23
k. Carer/personal assistant/support worker	2	0	1	2	1	2	0	1	1	3	25

A	B	C	D	E	F
16>	11–15	6–10	16>	11–15	6–10

(Typographic coding, as indicated below, has been used in the table above and in other similar multi-dimensional tables in this book to highlight strength of responses, indicating the numbers of people choosing a level of importance from highest to lowest for each source of advice or support highlighted. **A** represents very high or highest importance and is used for scores of 16 or above in the five left-hand columns, followed by **B** (scoring 11 to 15) and **C** (scoring 6 to 10). **D** represents very low or least importance and is used for scores of 16 or above in the five right hand columns, followed by **E** (11 to 15) and **F** (6 to 10)).

A little over a third (ten of twenty-eight) of respondents to a second survey within the Scottish 2015 study said that they would greatly value advice, information and support from an appropriately trained and experienced social worker or care worker on gender identity issues (Table 1.2, Norman, 2015a: p.221).

Table 1.2: The value of advice, information and support from an appropriately trained and experienced social worker or care worker regarding gender identity, and being transgender, through a better understanding of biological sex, (trans) gender identities and gender roles (Survey two: n = 29).

Valuation of advice, information and support in understanding gender identity, being transgender etc.	Number of respondents	Percentage of respondents
I would value this advice, information and support greatly	10	35
I would value this advice, information and support a little	3	11
I don't know how much I would value this advice, information and support	2	7
I would not value this advice, information and support very much	1	4
I would not value this advice, information and support at all	1	4
Not applicable: I do not need this advice, information and support	11	39
Total	**28**	**100**

Nine of these respondents were in the age groups 36–45 and 46–55. A three-way cross-tabulation with current gender role and gender identity indicated that all five of those in a female role who said that they would value support greatly described themselves as having a female gender identity. Similarly, three of the four people currently in a male gender role who also said they would value such support greatly had a male gender identity. These findings suggest that transition may not necessarily bring resolution to every issue relating to one's personal sense of gender identity or of being transgender. Seventeen of the twenty-eight respondents had either received such support in the past or were receiving it at present, from a social care or other source (Norman, 2015a, pp. 221–8).

One interviewee, Abigail, commented that she had never had a female or male identity and that she felt like she belonged neither to men nor to women. Such an ambiguity of gender was supported by responses offering the choice of 'as many as appropriate' gender descriptors: of the forty-seven respondents to the first survey of the Scottish 2015 study twenty-three people included 'transgender' among their preferences, with eight people including such terms as bi-gender, a-gender and poly-gender. Several frequently preferred combinations were evident: 'male/transgender/trans-man' appeared (sometimes in conjunction with other descriptors such as transsexual) on nine occasions. The combination of female and trans-woman appeared on ten occasions, six of which also included the term transsexual (Norman, 2015a, p. 216).

Transgender roles

Most transgender individuals (Whittle, 2000, p. 19) appear to recognise their transgender nature from an early age, and to share the 'passionate, lifelong, ineradicable conviction' (Morris, 1974, p. 15), present (even if not always discernible to others) from early childhood, to be accepted as a member of the opposite gender. Their initial journeys across the binary gender divide are usually short sojourns, testing the waters to explore the possibility of living permanently in the opposite binary gender role, with the assistance of hormonal and/or surgical interventions.

The perceived conflict described by many transgender people between their sense of their gender identity and the gender role to which they feel obliged to conform, which may be apparent through gender dysphoria, sheds a different light on the notion of gender than that portrayed by normative binary experiences and performative theory. Such a distinction between gender identity and role does not, however, necessarily conflict with theories of gender role conformity as a form of oppression. It may be reasonably argued that the experience of being 'trapped in the wrong body', often described by transgender people who seek to transition or to move beyond the binary, evidences a form of gender oppression within which enforced restriction to the 'wrong' binary gender role, or indeed to either binary gender role, may lead to severe psychological distress in the form of gender dysphoria.

Although Prosser refers to Bolin's (1996) contrast between 'transsexuality's conventional binary gendered past with the promise of a brave new transgendered binary-free future' (Prosser, 1998, p. 202) it seems more likely that there will be a gradual emergence of non-binary transgender people taking their place alongside the majority of those who transition to live within the opposite binary role. Bolin quotes the International Foundation for Gender Education which describes 'transgenderists' as 'persons who steer a middle course, living with the physical traits of both genders'. Although:

> they may alter their anatomy with hormones or surgery ... they may purposefully retain many of the characteristics of the gender to which they were originally assigned. Many lead part-time lives in both genders; most cultivate an androgynous appearance (Bolin, 1996, p. 466).

Within the Scottish 2015 study thirty-one of forty-seven participants identified with male (11) or female (20) gender identity categories while fourteen participants identified with transgender (9) or 'other' (5) categories. When respondents were able to indicate all of the gender descriptors with which they identified, there was a slightly greater likelihood for participants in younger age groups to describe themselves as transgender, while the term transsexual was less often chosen by biological females than biological males. Just four of the forty-seven respondents, all of whom were aged over forty-five years, saw themselves as falling within the category of 'cross-dresser, transvestite, drag queen, sissy or similar' (Norman, 2015a, pp. 214–17).

The gender dysphoria that many transgender people feel very early in their lives was readily apparent from the memories of childhood of two of the participants within the Scottish 2015 study, one of whom, Amy, indicated that she had been aware of her gender dysphoria from the age of seven, but it was only after suicidal thoughts that a visit to a GP began to help her to understand these feelings within the context of transsexuality (Norman, 2015a, p. 213). One respondent, Andrew, stated that 'I always knew I was different', and another, Suzie, spoke of 'gender confusion', while a survey correspondent stated that they thought that their gender identity was 'very possibly male still but it is complicated'. Suzie spoke of gender confusion, while a survey respondent thought that their gender identity was very possibly male but that it was complicated. The variance in these quotes suggests that there is a broad range of self-perceived difference, from doubt and uncertainty about one's gender status and the nature of the gendered relationship between oneself and others, to certainty that the nature of the problem lies in being 'trapped' in the wrong body (Norman, 2015a, pp. 211–219, 224, 330).

The maintenance of an initial gender role – individually nuanced perhaps, but apparently concordant with the multiplicity of behaviours which may be construed as 'normal' for one's assigned biological sex and gender, prior to transition – varied in duration from fourteen years to seventy-two years, with a mean of 34·3 and a median of 34·5 years. This suggests that gender dysphoria, the consequence of a conflict of gender identity and gender role, may be a long-term factor in many transgender people's lives (although, as the Scottish 2015 study also indicated, trending towards a shorter duration in FtM transgender people who appear more likely to transition at an earlier age (Norman, 2015a, pp. 135, 216, 220).

Such a conflict resulted in some participants taking a long time to understand their gender dysphoria: Andrew explained that he did not understand that he was transgender until he was thirty-nine, after seeing a documentary of a FtM person on TV. Several respondents commented about the difficulties of finding useful information online, and one, Ciaran, spoke of being confused by the limited information available. Gender dysphoria appeared particularly difficult to cope with during adolescence: one interviewee, Suzie, said that she had found the idea of puberty and its drastic effects on her future life to be both very confusing and upsetting (Norman, 2015a, pp. 115, 227, 321–2).

Transition and biological sex

Some research participants within the Scottish 2015 study felt that gender transition offered the possibility of altering at least one or more criteria of their biological sex, beyond the markers of social category (West and Zimmerman, 1987, p. 132). The survey participant who explained that their biological sex was female at birth, but that, having subsequently undergone gender reassignment from female to male, he no longer considered it accurate to say that his biological sex was simply female, raised a key aspect of gender transition: that it may alter some of the defining aspects of biological sex. More specifically, one interviewee, Josie, suggested that, having been on hormones for some twelve years, the chemical make-up of her body had significantly changed (Norman, 2015a, p. 211). The feminising and masculinising effects of the regular use of oestrogen by MtF transsexuals and of testosterone by FtM transsexuals are well documented (Seal, 2007, pp. 157–90).

One interviewee, Amy, was disappointed when she was not viewed consistently as a woman after transition, making it clear that she did not undertake 'the slow processes of transitioning to become a transsexual' (Norman, 2015a, pp. 218, 307). It seems that, despite the significant difficulties of the journey to date, some migrators may still be viewed (by some others) as essentially belonging to their original biological sex and, by implication, to their original gender (particularly so, perhaps, in the case of some MtF transgender people) (Whittle, 2000, pp. 49–50).

The participants of the Scottish 2015 study provided many examples of the profound conundrum at the heart of their gender dysphoria: how to resolve a gender identity/role conflict within a society that expects and reinforces conformity to the binary (Norman, 2015a). Lack of experience of gendered behaviours which are usually identified as corresponding to the transitioned binary gender may partially explain problems in passing, though these may also be linked with secondary sexual characteristics (including breast development (FtM) or vocal change (MtF)) resulting from puberty. It seems that, for some transgender people, seeking to resolve their conflict of gender identity through transitioning may result in trading the original deeply distressing personal dilemma of gender dysphoria for a similarly distressing, but more publicly evident conflict that centres on transitioned gendered appearance.

CHAPTER 2

Dedicated and Generic Social Care

Introduction

This chapter seeks to gauge progress in addressing the difficulties that transgender people may encounter when seeking support and empathy from dedicated and generic social care services, as they negotiate accommodation by and/or assimilation into contemporary society within male, female or transgender roles. Such difficulties are exacerbated by the implications of Mitchell and Howarth's finding, as recently as 2009, that there are 'no large scale surveys or research that focused specifically on the health and social care needs of the trans population' (Mitchell and Howarth, 2009, p. 62).

In addition, while the importance of some LGBT studies is noted below, some have proven disappointing, for, as Willis et al. suggest, 'the "T" is often included as a token gesture in the title of journal articles' (Willis et al., 2011, p. 1308). They draw a distinction between LGB and T needs by referencing the different circumstances of disclosure: for LGB people, coming out is a statement of affirmation of a potentially invisible sexual identity, while for transgender people it is a statement of affirmation of a gender identity which is continuously on display within gendered behaviour and presentation. The social care which each of these groups seeks is therefore likely to differ significantly, making the omission of transgender groups in some LGBT studies the more regrettable.

Transgender-related/generic social care and the role of advocacy

The provision of social care may be separated into dedicated or specialist care for transgender-related issues, and generic care which is usually provided to all members of society, albeit perhaps at different stages of their lives (although this may sometimes be gender specific: for example, support with domestic violence, which is primarily available to women).

Transgender-specific or dedicated social care may include assistance with coming to terms with a transgender identity, coping with transition-related issues within society, prior to, during or post-transition, and/or adjusting to the consequences of seeking to transcend the binary. A distinction must be recognised between those who transition and those who transcend. Davidson's analysis of transgender categories distinguishes between transsexual activists who seek to transition from one gender to another, and gender-queer individuals who attempt to break the conventions of the gender binary (Davidson, 2007, pp. 61–2). These two groups correspond closely to Ekins and King's 'migrators' and 'transcenders' respectively, to which they add the third category of 'oscillators', within which are included people who cross-dress but who always retain their sense of belonging to their original gender and biological sex (Ekins and King, 2006, pp. 43, 97, 181).

A further specific role of social care agencies might be to include information sharing and advocacy to promote a greater awareness of the needs of transgender people. Indeed, Burdge argues that it is the responsibility of 'social workers to target society's traditional gender dichotomy for change' while nonetheless noting an apparent absence of action 'to strike gender-based oppression at its heart by challenging the gender binary' (Burdge, 2007, pp. 243, 246). That binary oppression affects those who seek to transition is highlighted by Taylor, who within 'an exploration of ethical social work practice' found that, when transmen respondents 'did not fit into traditional gender roles, they reported being labelled as "less deserving" of interventions surrounding their gender identity'. Taylor concludes that 'social workers have an ethical responsibility to … move towards models of care that expand understanding of gender to include a transgender analysis of gender diversity' (Taylor, 2013, pp. 116, 118).

Generic social care, on the other hand, may involve support related to accommodation (homelessness, care at home, residential or nursing care), welfare benefits, substance addiction, the criminal justice system, mental illness, physical or learning disability, and domestic or societal abuse. While transgender people may indeed use these services, they are not trans-specific and may affect many people in society, particularly if they belong to a minority or disadvantaged group. Cruz found that more than 50% of transgender people delay seeking healthcare, compared to 20% of the general population, suggesting that the reasons for such avoidance appear to reflect a link between increased visibility and increased levels of direct discrimination (Cruz, 2014, p. 71). It might be reasonably hypothesised that such a delay may affect the timescales for those seeking social care too.

Discrimination and exclusion within social care services

It is not difficult to find evidence in recent academic publications relating to discrimination against transgender people within health settings (see, for example, Whittle *et al.*, 2007), although figures relating to social care settings are less easy to identify.

In 2013 Stotzer *et al.*, for example, analysed 105 articles from 1995 to 2011 on 'barriers to care' ... 'pertaining to the social situation, health and mental health of transgender people', of which only thirty had 'specific content related to transgender peoples' experiences in social service settings' (Stotzer *et al.*, 2013, p. 66). Furthermore, because their definition of social service settings ranged from 'medical care to housing', traditional social care services form a much smaller proportion of these thirty services than might be anticipated. However, their findings highlight significant discrimination within those generic social care services that they looked at, including access to accommodation within homeless shelters, discrimination in child custody determinations, exclusion from drug treatment programmes (with inclusion only if participants dressed in the clothes, and showered and slept in facilities associated with their biological sex), access to mental health support, difficulties with claiming welfare benefits, and a general absence of transgender-appropriate intake forms (Stotzer *et al.*, 2013, pp. 67–72).

Stotzer *et al.*'s review contains no mention of how attitudes to transgender people affect care-at-home services and residential and nursing care, though these had been the subject of earlier LGBT research. Cartwright *et al.*, for example, in a scoping report on end-of-life care for elderly gay, lesbian, bisexual and transgender people reported how:

> Discrimination or anticipated discrimination was also reported as preventing access to health care. Service providers observed that, in a small town, clients who could access services locally chose not to in order to protect their privacy and identity. Some travelled to other areas but others just missed out. Further,

community participants spoke about how some GLBT people chose to live on the margins of society, for example in self-sufficient rural communities, to avoid the confrontation of discrimination in the mainstream heterosexual and heterosexist world. Participants believed both decisions resulted in failures to access advance care planning and quality end-of-life care when it was needed (Cartwright *et al.*, 2012 p. 11).

Similarly, Addis *et al.* in a meta-analysis of 187 papers or chapters on the health, social care and housing needs of older lesbian, gay, bisexual and transgender adults found that:

the main themes that emerge from the review were isolation (and that) the health, social care and housing needs of LGBT older people is (*sic*) influenced by a number of forms of discrimination which may impact upon … provision and access (Addis *et al.*, 2009, p. 647).

Discrimination may also be found within dedicated transgender services. Stotzer *et al.* identified reports where respondents had been refused counselling (including counselling for transgender-related issues) because they were transgender, amid concerns about insensitive treatment, as well as the absence of trans-specific social services and programmes, particularly for those not living in large urban environments (Stotzer *et al.*, 2013, pp. 67–72). The Scottish 2015 study indicated that transgender people in Scotland had restricted access to local support groups because of geographical issues and their limited availability, a concern highlighted by both voluntary and statutory sector respondents (Norman, 2015a, p. 183), despite increasing recognition that 'support groups offer a key source of care within transgender communities' (Hines, 2007, p. 483).

Awareness of transgender need

Siverskog found that older transgender interviewees (aged 62–78) had experienced a lack of knowledge about trans issues, even within the transition process, among staff who worked specifically with trans patients, and concerns about prejudice were also evident. One of her interviewees, for example, 'expressed a fear that caregivers would see her as "disgusting" and refuse to give her care' (Siverskog, 2014, pp. 391, 397).

While Stotzer *et al.* did not distinguish between statutory and voluntary providers of social care services, they noted that LGB providers (who were more likely to be from within the voluntary sector) did not necessarily understand the needs of transgender people, and that the needs of LGB people may be prioritised within LGBT support services (Stotzer *et al.,* 2013, p. 68). For those transgender individuals who are able to attend support groups, it seems from the Scottish 2015 study that other transgender people may become close confidantes and, within such relationships, the expression of need and the provision of support are likely to be informal and largely based on trust (Norman, 2015a, pp. 177–83, 237).

The Scottish 2015 study also indicated that dedicated transgender voluntary organisations were more likely to be aware of local transgender service provision than statutory sector organisations, and that voluntary organisations also showed more awareness of areas of outstanding need. Most local support, even from within the voluntary sector sample, was provided to transgender adults: there was only a little evidence of transgender children/young people receiving support, while family members, including partners/children of transgender adults and parents of transgender children/young people also appeared to receive limited local support. In addition to these gaps in the service, telephone support was identified as a necessary additional service, perhaps reinforcing the importance of anonymity: a person seeking initial advice and support about being part of a marginalised, abused and stigmatised group might prefer the lack of personal identification that telephone contact offers, while seeking levels of individualised support that online forums may struggle to emulate (Norman, 2015a, pp. 177–83).

Equality and policy statements and staff training

Stotzer *et al.* note that it is 'critical to have clear policy statements' regarding anti-discrimination and fair treatment, and that 'agencies need to think critically about when to offer transgender specific programs and when to integrate transgender people into existing services' (Stotzer *et al.,* 2013, p. 74). The Scottish 2015 study indicated that policy statements were largely absent for both generic and dedicated/specialist services in Scotland according to the twelve statutory and eight voluntary sector respondents, and that those policy statements and equality action plans that were in place tended towards generalised statements rather than being specifically linked to transgender need. No evidence was found that written guidelines/guidance for staff providing dedicated/specialist service provision to transgender people were in place for any of the statutory or voluntary organisations represented by respondents (Norman, 2015a, p. 195).

Stotzer *et al.* conclude their article by suggesting that 'agencies and programmes can easily make climates more hospitable for transgender people … by providing transgender-specific information pamphlets' etc. and by 'demonstrating a welcoming atmosphere to transgender clients' (Stotzer *et al.*, 2013, p. 74). However, Concannon suggests that 'creating anti-oppressive practices in service provision that successfully remove barriers to the social inclusion of older lesbians, gay men, bisexual and transgendered citizens has proven thus far tremendously difficult'. He notes 'the unique oppression and marginalisation' that these groups face, and suggests the development of social policy strategies (consultation forums, training packages, advocacy, equal opportunity policies etc.) to include these groups in service planning and delivery (Concannon, 2009, p. 403). He refers to the Sexual Orientation and Gender Identity Advisory Group, the Department of Health forum for LGBT engagement between 2005 and 2009, where, however, the needs of transgender people are somewhat overshadowed by those of GLB people in all but one of the seventeen briefing papers and publications produced by this advisory group (Stonewall, 2015).

The Scottish 2015 study into social care service provision to transgender people identified only a very few examples of diversity training on transgender issues or of targeted training to frontline staff at access points for social care service users. Statutory staff had received more training in working with transgender people than their voluntary-sector counterparts; dedicated/specialist staff at half of the voluntary organisations had received no training in transgender issues at all (Norman, 2015a, pp. 191–4). Tolley and Ranzijn, in a 'study of heteronormativity amongst staff of residential aged care facilities', found that 'increased exposure to gay and lesbian people was directly related to … (increased knowledge) and also to reduced heterosexism' (Tolley and Ranzijn, 2006, p. 83). It is anticipated that a similar reduction in transphobia might be found as care staffs' knowledge of transgender identities increases through targeted training and experience.

Lastly, Stotzer *et al.* note the importance of influencing 'the attitudes and behaviours of non-transgender clients' (Stotzer *et al.,* 2013, p. 74) to transgender people. One of the (service provider) interviewees to the Scottish 2015 study presented a valuable perspective on how transgender people might be viewed by service providers and other service users, particularly in 'single sex' services, and how this might impact on access to such services. Her belief that 'the binary view of gender is more related to an "ease" by which services can ... be developed ... according to male/female aspects of gender' (Norman, 2015a, p. 329) is a point of view that Siverskog's interviewees appear to acknowledge when she notes that 'care and social services were perceived as not being created for the clients, but ... for a policing of genders and bodies' (Siverskog, 2014, p. 397).

'Core values' and social care provision

The interviewee from the Scottish 2015 study quoted above who commented on the normativity of gender boundaries in service provision went on to suggest that 'some service providers may feel that, whilst a transgender woman presents physically as a woman, their core values are related to their biological sex and gendered early years' (Norman, 2015a, p. 329). There is an absence of research to define and explore the notion of gendered 'core values' and, if these can be consistently identified, the degree to which these are assimilated by transgender people during their formative years. In addition, there is also a vacuum in research into the degree to which transition might affect or alter such core values, perhaps through expressed changes in attitudes and interests by altered gendered behaviour within personal relationships and friendships, and within the nature and composition of close social networks.

Similarly, despite the insistence by some feminist writers (e.g. Greer, 2015) that MtF transgender people are not women (and, by implication, that FtM transgender people are not men) there is an absence of research into the degree to which these views are shared by the wider public. The 2006 Scottish Social Attitudes Survey (SSAS) Main Findings from 1,594 interviewees across Scotland did, however, indicate that 50% of respondents 'would be unhappy about a relative forming a long-term relationship with a transsexual person' (Bromley *et al.,* 2007, p. 15).

It is possible that some of these views may be derived from limited knowledge of transgender matters: Siverskog's interviewees, for example, found themselves repeatedly having to 'explain themselves, educate others, and dismantle misconceptions of what transgender means' (Siverskog, 2014, p. 396), while, reassuringly, the SSAS also found that 'those who know someone who belongs to a particular group are less likely to express discriminatory attitudes' (Bromley *et al.*, 2007).

By 2010 the percentage of people who said that they would be unhappy at the prospect of a close relative forming a relationship with 'someone who had had a sex change operation' was 49%, a very small change since the 50% figure of 2006 (Ormston *et al.*, 2011, p. 71). However, the most recent updates from the SSAS, based on their 2015 survey, suggest that while there are still concerns – 39% of respondents said that they would be unhappy about someone who cross-dresses in public marrying a close relative – a drop from 49% to 32% was found for those who would be concerned by someone who has undergone gender reassignment marrying a close relative – significant progress in just five years (Scottish Government, 2016, p. 23).

Incidence and levels of transgender need

One of the difficulties of providing social care to transgender people involves the estimation of incidence of transgender people in the community, and of their levels of need. As one of the statutory organisation respondents to the Scottish 2015 study acknowledged: 'We don't even know how many transgender people are within our population' (Norman, 2015a, p. 154). Another respondent commented that 'given that I work in a small authority with a small population … it would be beneficial for three or four authorities to work together to provide dedicated specialised services for transgender people and their families' (Norman, 2015a, p. 184).

The most accurate direct estimate of incidence of transsexual people in Scotland used the parameters of Wilson *et al.*'s (1999) survey data, and was based on doctors' knowledge of transgender patients who had presented with gender dysphoria, of which there were 429 (one in 12,225) individuals. Ten years later, GIRES' figure of one in 5,000 individuals within the UK (Reed *et al.*, 2009, p. 4) was based on a presumed prevalence, taking into account an estimated 6,000 who had undertaken transition. GIRES' current website provides information that 'about 26,000 individuals have so far sought medical care, in general practice or specialist centres' (within the UK) (GIRES, 2015a).

Lastly GIRES most recent online posting (GIRES, 2015b) provides a detailed breakdown of revised estimates originally supplied to the Home Office, indicating a range of levels of incidence in the UK:

- gender non-conforming to some degree: 1% – one in 100;
- likely to seek medical treatment for their condition at some stage: 0.2% – one in 500;
- receiving such treatment already: 0.03% – one in 3,300;
- having already undergone transition: 0.02% – one in 5,000;
- having a gender reassignment certificate: 0.005% – one in 20,000.

While it is important to stress that these are estimates, with background information on their sources not included on the GIRES website, they do appear to confirm a steady increase in the incidence of transgender people seeking assistance in the UK, for whom social care may be needed. In addition, very recent figures 'reveal increases in referrals to all of the UK's gender identity clinics (GICs) in recent years, with a number of clinics experiencing increases of several hundred percent' (*The Guardian*, 2016a).

CHAPTER 3

Gender Transitions

Introduction

For most men or women the notion of undertaking a journey from one gender role to another might seem inexplicable – why put at risk the social status associated with one's biological sex and original gender role, painstakingly developed over a lifetime, opening up the very real possibility of rejection by family, friends, colleagues, neighbours, acquaintances and wider society? Jan Morris' concept of an 'ineradicable conviction' (Morris, 1974, p. 15) of a sense of incongruity, of belonging to a different gender than the one initially assigned, often summarised as being 'in the wrong body' gives some notion of the depth of this need to change. Jeanette Winterson entitled her autobiography *Why Be Happy When You Could Be Normal?* reflecting the response of her mother when she explained her lesbianism to her (Winterson, 2011). The parallels with the search for conflict resolution by many transgender people seem evident – one can continue living a 'normal' life, hiding and sublimating one's inner conflict, or one can seek an inner happiness, despite the likely change to an established social status, by coming out and by transitioning, very much in the public eye.

Migratory categories

Many transgender writings describe an incompatibility between inner gender identity and outer gender role and biological sex. Jeffreys, however, notes that 'women do not 'define' their gender identity' (Jeffreys, 2014, p. 145), and one suspects that the vast majority of men do not consciously do so either, for gender identity appears so inextricably bound up with who we are and the social roles of everyday life designated according to biological sex, that few perhaps feel the need to question or even consider it. But, as Erhardt explains, the condition of gender dysphoria in a transgender person is an involuntary one (Erhardt, 2007, p. 6) that often appears very early in life, and one for which the transgender person has few choices other than how to deal with a conflict that affects almost every aspect of daily life.

For some at least, the choice of matching inner gender identity with gender role becomes an increasingly necessary and even inevitable option for the resolution of an otherwise lifelong internal discordance, albeit at the risk of isolation and rejection. Those whose new gender role is the subject of such rejection may take some comfort from Goffman's observation, in a broader discussion of stigma, that:

> it is very difficult to understand how individuals who sustain a sudden transformation of their life from that of a 'normal' to that of a stigmatised person can survive the change psychologically; yet very often they do (Goffman, 1968, p. 158).

As noted in the previous chapter, it is difficult to know how many transgender people there are within a population, not least because many do not make their condition known, and it is therefore unclear what percentage of this minority population choose to transition to match their gender role to their gender identity. Rosser *et al.*'s Internet study of 1,229 members of a non-clinical transgender population in the United States indicated that a little under half of them were migrators (44%), almost a fifth were oscillators (18%), almost a third categorised themselves as 'other' (29%), while a further 9% described themselves as drag queens or drag kings (Rosser *et al.*, 2007, p. 58).

In contrast, somewhat over a half (twenty-seven of forty-seven) of respondents to the Scottish 2015 study, drawn from the membership of the Scottish Transgender Alliance (STA), said that they had already changed their gender role to match their gender identity. Of these twenty-seven individuals thirteen biological males, five biological females and five who described themselves as of 'other' or unspecified biological sex had completed transitions to the (in the main) alternative binary gender role. Some migrators had, however, chosen a non-binary destination: two biological males and one biological female said that they had developed a gender role that reflected a bi-gender identity as both male and female, while one intersex person stated that they had developed a gender role to reflect their androgyne gender identity (indicating a total of just four 'transcenders' within forty-seven (9%) participants of the survey) (Norman, 2015a, p. 219).

In addition, six biological males and three biological females were in the process of transition, and two of each biological sex said that they would like to change their gender role to match their gender identity, giving a total of forty of forty-seven people (85%) who indicated that they fell within a 'migrating' category. Two participants indicated that they were 'happy to spend some time in the opposite gender role' but did not want to do this permanently (indicating very few participants who identified as cross-dressers), while five described themselves as 'other' (Norman, 2015a, p. 230).

Age, sex and transition

Rosser *et al.* indicate that the mean age of MtF and FtM migratory trans-sexuals who responded to their survey differed at 37.2 (n = 278) and 28 (n = 262) respectively (Rosser *et al.*, 2007, p. 58). Within the Scottish 2015 study biological males outnumbered biological females over the age of forty-six by 21:1, with biological females outnumbering biological males in the age group 16–25 by 6:1 suggesting an emerging group of younger FtM transgender people (Norman, 2015a, p. 206) that appears to correspond with GIRES' prediction of a more equal MtF/FtM balance in time within the UK (Reed *et al.*, 2009, p. 17). There was a fairly even spread across age ranges 16–25 through to 60+, of those who were in the process of a gender role change, with those in the younger age ranges being predominantly biologically female (Norman, 2015a, p. 206).

The period spent in transitioned gender roles, with a mean of 7.3 and a median of five years, was relatively short compared to the period spent in the original gender role. In the context of gender as a 'condition actively under construction' (Connell, 2009, p. 5), these figures indicate that for many migrating transgender people experience in the transitioned gender role (particularly for those who transitioned later in life) was significantly less than that within their original gender role (Norman, 2015a, p. 221).

The real-life test/experience

Barrett explains that the real-life test is a consequence of a requirement of health services in the UK for a minimum of one year to be spent successfully living in the transition role prior to gender reassignment/ confirmation surgery, which is largely irreversible. He distinguishes between such a time-limited 'real life test' and the 'real life experience', which 'is very likely to last the remainder of the patient's days'. Some gatekeepers to NHS-funded surgery require a longer test period – the Charing Cross Hospital requires migrators to live in their chosen role for two years. Private surgery is less likely to require any test period (Barrett, 2007, pp. 71–3).

Doan argues that 'gender transitions are never private affairs; by design they occur in ... and provide a different lens with which to view the gendering of public spaces' (Doan, 2010, p. 640). Barrett defines success in living in a chosen gender role as 'occupational, sexual, relationship and psychological stability', and goes on to explain that clarification of the degree to which a patient is 'passing' (both within their preferred gender, and the test itself) may be ascertained simply by the likelihood that a stranger would 'address the patient as male or female' (Barrett, 2007, p. 72).

Whittle's (2008) paper provides useful guidelines for changing a range of documents within banks, health services, government agencies, etc. In some cases these are relatively straightforward, particularly if a letter of support from a doctor confirms that the change is intended to be permanent. The issuing of a GRC may make any future name changes more straightforward, but Whittle is clear that a GRC 'is never required for a lawful change of names and gender pronouns for trans people' (Whittle, 2008, p. 3). As a transgender person needs to live in the transition role for a full two years before an application for a GRC can be made, the provision of a GRC is, therefore, of little relevance to documentation changes during the real-life test.

Twenty-nine respondents to the Scottish 2015 study had undertaken the twelve-month real-life test. Eight of these were now living in a male gender role, eighteen in a female gender role, and three in a transgender role. As one interviewee noted, the consequences of the test were very significant:

> **Abigail**: I began the process called 'the real life test' – in which you are supposed to start living full time as a woman. This has the hugest implications in every aspect of your life, again, without support. Anything, absolutely anything, would have been welcome' (Norman, 2015a, p. 233).

None of the respondents had undertaken this test and not completed it, or had completed it and then reverted to living in their original gender role. The finding that six people (five of whom were in the predominantly biologically female age groups 16–25 or 26–35) had undertaken gender role reassignment without undertaking a real-life test raises the possibility that some younger transgender people were transitioning without meeting this GIC requirement, and, therefore, had done so without GIC support. Cross-tabulating age with 'real life experience' indicated that there was a tendency for an increase in the numbers of (mainly biologically male) participants who had undertaken this step as part of gender-role reassignment, as age increased, through age groups 26–35 (three of eight), 36–45 (seven of nine), up to age group 46–55 (ten of eleven) (Norman, 2015a, p. 233).

Undertaking a transition

Often within a short period of time and with little opportunity to practise the presentation and performance of the gender of transition, a transgender person, if they are to feel comfortable and 'pass', needs to consider and adjust speech and use of language, as well as aspects of appearance such as clothing, hair-style and posture. As importantly, they will need to consider how these changes will affect their social role and status within their family, their network of friends, their educational establishment or their employment, and within their local community and wider society.

This very brief summary of some of the issues which both MtF and FtM transgender people might need to consider at the time of transition inevitably fails to encompass the wide range of subtle behaviour that people who have lived a lifetime in one gender or the other have learned to display, elicit and accommodate, and which need to be quickly mastered if such newly learned behaviours are to be rendered acceptable within contemporary expectations for the adopted gender role. These behaviours and expectations are likely to vary within the company of men, women, transgender people or in groups of mixed gender (and/or mixed ages etc.), and within the varying degrees of intimacy that define and clarify relationships and interactions with those that feel closest and those that seem most superficial – further complicated, too, by notions of sexuality and sexual attraction. While notions of passing and visibility are widely raised and discussed on transgender forums (e.g. Reddit, 2016), more nuanced notions of social acceptance (including, for example, intimacy within personal friendships and relationships) are less commonly explored.

Brown and Rounsley neatly summarise this process when they suggest that a transgender person 'cannot simply emerge "full blown" as the other gender. They must rebuild themselves psychologically, socially and inter-personally' (Brown and Rounsley, 2003, p. 127). It may seem surprising then that medical interventions are so strongly prioritised over social care support to transgender people – and to their families and friends – prior to, before and after transition, although as Davidmann notes: 'medical inter-est in transsexuality developed upon the principle that genital surgery is fundamental to transsexual identities' (Davidmann, 2010, p. 188).

Social care support is particularly pertinent at around the time of puberty when physical changes and their emotional consequences are at their most intense. However, it may also be argued that older transgender people have to 'undo or unlearn' the more complex con-sequences of living for a longer period within their original assigned gender role: social care support may also assist in the 'unpicking' of former identities (and perhaps core values), behaviour and roles.

Billings and Urban argue that the anxieties and difficulties that many migrating transgender people experience in seeking to be accepted within their local or wider community suggest (Billings and Urban, 1996, p. 114):

> that Meyer and Hoopes were correct when they wrote that, 'in a thousand subtle ways the reassignee has the bitter experience that he (*sic*) is not – and never will be – a real girl, but is, at best a convincing simulated female. Such an adjustment cannot compensate for the tragedy of having lost all chance to be male, and of having in the final analysis, no way to be really female' (Meyer and Hoopes, 1974, p. 450).

Such a perspective on the 'tragedy of having lost all chance to be male', and what it means to be 'really female' shows no empathy for the transgender person's dilemma, reflected within extensive research that finds that transgender people experience and live with the con-sequences of gender dysphoria almost without exception from a very early age (see, for example, Whittle, 2000, p. 19; Kennedy and Hellen, 2010, p. 28). Nor does it show any recognition of the artificiality of the social construction of male and female roles within society or successful attempts by those transgender people who bridge and who find a niche within or outwith male and female binary roles.

Nonetheless, transgender people may experience difficulty in understanding their own gender and transgender status, and in undertaking their complex personal journeys of transition. Despite the complexities of finding a valued place within an – at times at least – antipathetic and sometimes hostile world, there is, however, very little evidence of serious regret at transitions undertaken, or of serious disappointment with the outcomes of a life journey with which many who do not need to question the link between their biological sex and their male or female identity and gender role might find it hard to empathise (see also the Follow-up studies section in Chapter 5).

Sources of support during a transition

Within the Scottish 2015 study, close friends were rated of highest importance by twelve respondents as a source of support regarding transition, although eleven respondents viewed their close friends as being of lowest importance, too. However, almost twice the number of these participants rated friends in the three highest importance columns than the three columns of lowest importance, suggesting that this is likely to be a strong source of support to the majority of those transitioning (Table 3.1; Norman, 2015a, pp. 235–6).

Further analysis through a three-way cross-tabulation indicated that eight of the ten respondents in a current male gender role and with a male gender identity rated close friends in the three highest categories for support with transition issues (with just one of these respondents viewing close friends in the three lowest categories for such support). Conversely, of the fourteen respondents in a current female gender role, and with a female gender identity, only seven considered close friends in the three highest categories for support with transition issues, with four respondents placing them in the three lowest categories. These findings concur with additional data from within the Scottish 2015 study, which indicated a tendency for friends to be rated less highly for support with gender identity issues by MtF than by FtM people (Table 1.1; Norman, 2015a, pp. 221–8).

Whittle *et al.*'s (2007, p. 69) evidence of limitations within family support appears to be illustrated by the finding within the Scottish 2015 study that family members were considered of least importance by ten partici-

Table 3.1: The importance of sources of advice or support in helping to undertake transition (Survey one: n = 47: 40 respondents).

Key: Importance of sources of advice and support regarding gender role transition (1 = highest importance, 11 = least importance).

Source/Importance of advice or support in helping to undertake transition	1	2	3	4	5	6	7	8	9	10	11
a. Close friends	12	3	6	1	2	2	0	0	1	0	11
b. Family members	6	7	3	2	2	2	3	3	0	1	10
c. Colleagues at work /line manager	3	2	4	3	2	3	1	2	1	3	12
d. Transgender support group	14	3	6	2	1	1	2	0	1	2	5
e. General practitioner	4	6	4	1	6	5	1	0	2	1	8
f. Gender specialist at GIC	10	3	4	3	3	1	1	3	1	2	9
g. Speech therapist	6	0	3	2	0	3	2	4	1	2	11
h. Health visitor or district nurse	1	0	0	0	1	2	0	2	2	4	22
i. Counsellor or psychiatrist	6	4	5	1	4	2	3	0	0	4	8
j. Social worker	2	0	0	1	1	1	1	1	4	2	20
k. Carer/personal assistant/support worker	2	1	1	0	0	1	2	0	0	4	22

A	B	C	D	E	F
16>	11–15	6–10	16>	11–15	6–10

For full explanation of typographic coding, please see table 1.1 on p.13.

pants as a source of advice or support during transition, whereas just six rated them as of the highest importance. However, overall, rather more family members were placed in the three highest categories of importance than within the three lowest categories of lower importance (Table 3.1).

A three-way cross-tabulation of the research data indicated that eight of the ten respondents in a current male gender role and with a male gender identity viewed family members in the three highest categories for support with transition issues (with just one respondent placing family members in the three lowest categories for such support). Conversely, of the four-teen respondents in a current female gender role, and with a female gender identity, just two rated family members in the three highest categories, with four respondents placing them in the three lowest categories (Norman, 2015a, pp. 236–7). These findings reinforce the tendency for family members to be viewed less highly for support with gender identity issues by MtF than by FtM people (Table 1.1; Norman, 2015a, pp. 221–8).

Transgender support groups were rated within the three categories of highest importance by more than half (twenty-three of forty) of respondents as a source of advice regarding making a transition, but with eight people placing them within the three least important categories too (Table 3.1). Members of support groups were perhaps most likely to have under-taken gender reassignment/confirmation themselves, and may well have been able to show a valuable degree of empathy and compassion for other transgender people at a very vulnerable time in their lives. A comment from one transgender interviewee evidenced their willingness to provide such support to others:

> **Amy:** 'I still attend my gender support group meeting ... to help others in their transition as I can answer any questions about gender reassignment surgery (Norman, 2015a, p. 238).

It was noted, however, that not all respondents had access to such groups:

> **Ciaran:** 'I would have liked to (have) been able to speak to someone further into their transition but after a few bad experiences online seeking fellow trans-people I'd now rather get on with things the best I can ... since I started my transformation ... I have still never met another trans-man or trans- woman' (Norman, 2015a, p. 238).

A three-way cross-tabulation indicated that seven of the nine respondents in a current male gender role and with a male gender identity rated transgender support groups in the three highest categories for support with transition issues (with none of these respondents placing transgender support groups in the three lowest categories for such support). But of the thirteen respondents in a current female gender role, and with a female gender identity, only six individuals considered transgender support groups as being in the three highest categories, with four respondents viewing them in the three lowest categories, reflecting similar differences regarding support from transgender support groups to MtF and FtM individuals with gender identity issues (Norman, 2015a, pp. 221–8, 237); once again, the reasons for the disparity are unclear.

A quarter of the forty respondents rated gender specialists at a GIC as their most highly valued source of support regarding helping to undertake a transition, and overall more respondents considered them of higher than of lower importance, although nine viewed them as their least valued source of support (Norman, 2015a, p. 238). One reason for this was touched on by one interviewee who commented:

> **Sarah**: 'Ten weeks of support during a transition process that can take years is not a significant amount of contact over a long enough period.' (Norman, 2015a, p.239)

Another interviewee observed:

> **Luke**: 'An appointment roughly every six months at times hasn't been sufficient' (Norman, 2015a, p.239)

Another interviewee commented on the difficulties of accessing their GIC and surgical facilities:

> **Ciaran**: 'It's not ideal that my nearest GIC involves a 200 -mile round trip and I have to travel to London for operations' (Norman, 2015a, p. 239).

A three-way cross-tabulation indicated that three of the ten respondents in a current male gender role and with a male gender identity rated the GIC in the three highest categories for support with transition issues (but with just one respondent placing the GIC in the three lowest categories for such support), confirming the suggestion above that fewer FtM migrants may use the GIC route during their transition. In contrast, of the fourteen respondents in a current female gender role, and with a female gender identity, seven rated the GIC in the three highest categories, but with four respondents placing them in the three lowest categories (Norman, 2015a, p. 238).

A further three-way cross-tabulation also indicated that just three of the ten respondents in a current male gender role and with a male gender identity placed counsellors or psychiatrists in the three highest categories for support with transition issues (with three respondents also rating counsellors or psychiatrists in the three lowest categories for such support). Conversely, of the fourteen respondents in a current female gender role, and with a female gender identity, eight considered counsellors or psychiatrists to be in the three highest categories, with just three respondents rating them in the three lowest categories (Norman, 2015a, pp. 238–9).

It appears then that FtM individuals, as well as being more likely to be within a younger age group, were rather more likely to find sources of support from friends, family or transgender support groups and less likely to seek support from a GIC or counsellors or psychiatrists compared to the very different, almost converse situation for MtF people.

Table 3.1 also indicates that twice as many GPs were considered of least importance (eight) in helping to make a transition as those who were viewed of highest importance (four), highlighting Whittle *et al.*'s finding that 21% of GPs did not want to help transgender people (Whittle *et al.*, 2007, p. 16). However, fourteen respondents rated GPs in the three highest importance columns, with eleven placing them in the three columns of lowest importance.

Although it appears that only a few participants felt that their workplace was a strong source of advice and support (Table 3.1), with almost twice as many placing them in the three lowest categories of support, for some transgender people, transition was greatly aided by support from work colleagues:

> **Kay:** 'Both my work and friends have been wonderful. They are not knowledgeable on transgender at all, and so can't help in that respect, but the support, encouragement and warmth has been desperately critical, especially from work. I feel much sympathy for folk without this support' (Norman, 2015a, p. 241).

Social care support during a transition

The value of support from a social or care worker to help transgender people during a gender role transition or the real-life test was also explored within the Scottish 2015 study (Norman, 2015a, pp. 240–4). This indicated that ten (37%) of twenty-seven participants would greatly value assistance from an appropriately trained and experienced social worker or care worker during a gender role transition or the real-life test, with a further four participants saying that they would value this a little. The same number (ten, 37%) of participants said that they did not need such assistance (Table 3.2).

Table 3.2: The value of advice, information and support from an appropriately trained and experienced social worker or care worker during a gender role transition or the 'real life test' (Survey two: n = 29).

Valuation of advice, information and support during a gender role transition or 'real life test'	Number of respondents	Percentage of respondents
I would value this advice, information and support greatly	10	37
I would value this advice, information and support a little	4	15
I don't know how much I would value this advice, information and support	2	7
I would not value this advice, information and support very much	1	4
I would not value this advice, information and support at all	0	0
Not applicable: I do not need this advice, information and support	10	37
Total	**27**	**100**

One interviewee explained that such a support role might also be helpful during the waiting period before transition, when GIC support was not yet available.

> **Kay**: 'An experienced social worker or care worker during this waiting period could have provided advice at least, and even just the emotional support so as not to feel isolated' (Norman, 2015a, p. 242).

Another interviewee explained why a social worker perspective would be helpful for what is often viewed essentially as a medical process:

> **Lucy:** 'I think a trained social worker would be a good step as a means of de-medicalising our condition. It is something that should be out in the community and not in a doctor's surgery. It is all about life skills and choices. Sure you need a medical input for some things like hormones; however a good social worker is every bit as good and a lot less tarred with the medical brush' (Norman, 2015a, p. 356).

In total, seven of twenty-seven respondents had received such support during a transition in the past, from a social or care worker, or from another source. Just three participants indicated that they were receiving such support at present (Norman, 2015a, p. 242).

Of the ten people who said that they would value advice and support greatly during a gender transition, six were currently in a female role, three in a male and one in a transgender role. A three-way cross-tabulation indicated that five of the six people in a female role and one of the three in a male role had actually already made the transition from the opposite binary role, suggesting that the transition process may be long and complex, particularly for those who are MtF, for whom advice and support may be needed for some time after the initial 'transformation'. This may also be the case for those who adopt an alternative gender role outwith the binary (Norman, 2015a, p. 242).

It seems from the findings summarised in the last two sections of this chapter, that the social care needs and sources of support for migrating transgender people may vary according to biological sex, and may be partly linked with a difference in the likely age of transition between individuals within the two groups. Such differences may be further exacerbated by the apparently differing responses of society to migrating MtF and FtM people, and this is one of the issues that will be explored within the next chapter, in a consideration of discrimination and transphobia.

CHAPTER 4

Discrimination and Transphobia

Introduction

Non-acceptance or failure to pass successfully in a transitioned role may result in very punitive responses to transgender people. Such experiences provide very negative feedback to transgender people, very different from the feedback that the majority of people who grow up in a gender role that matches their gender identity are likely to receive. It is possible that a deficit in information on transgender issues may reinforce both misunderstanding and ignorance, which may be the precursors of prejudice, discrimination and transphobia.

This chapter will explore some of these underpinning issues and the potential for rejection within family, friends, neighbours, colleagues etc. to a transgender person with whom they have a relationship, and the wider community who may not know a transgender individual but who become aware of transgender people through, for example, increasing media exposure.

Transphobia

Several instances of transphobia were noted within the responses of survey participants and interviewees from the Scottish 2015 study. For example, one interviewee, Ciaran, stated that he was assaulted more than once (Norman, 2015a, p. 279) while another, Lucy, described how she was refused service in shops because of her gender change (Norman, 2015a, p. 298).

There were also examples of less abusive, but nonetheless disabling responses: for example, where participants lost contact with relatives because of their transgender status, sometimes at the expense of other family relationships. Luke spoke of how his mother, in particular, found his transition very hard, especially in view of the rejection from his uncle and his wife, who ignored him at family gatherings. Another interviewee, Sarah, explained that, with the exception of her mother, her family appeared not to want to acknowledge her as a family member (Norman, 2015a, pp. 260–1): family relationships are discussed in more detail in chapter six below.

As Goffman suggests, in a broader discussion of the relationship between stigma and the 'discrediting' of social groupings, it is likely that there may be 'no open recognition to what is discrediting' (Goffman, 1968, p. 57), so that a lack of eye contact or avoidance of personal contact or conversely an unfriendly glance or stare, an inappropriate comment or joke in a public setting, poor service in a shop (or within one's home or over the telephone) might be intended and/or perceived as discriminatory or transphobic. Such apparently 'trivial' incidents are likely to be recognised as fairly common by transgender people (and other minority groups that are discriminated against) but they receive far less attention than the significantly more disabling examples of blatant transphobia which can be found within the research literature. The STA survey of seventy-one transgender people in Scotland in 2007, which looked at more overt forms of discrimination, found that 62% of respondents had suffered harassment from strangers, mostly in 'the form of verbal abuse, with 31% experiencing threatening behaviour, 17% experiencing physical assault and 4% experiencing sexual assault' (Morton, 2008, pp. 11–18). Similarly, the Equalities Review 'Engendered Penalties' (based on a 2006 survey of 873 individuals and supplementary data from Press for Change and the FtM Network from 1998 to 2005) reported that '73% of (transgender and transsexual) respondents experienced comments, threatening behaviour, physical abuse, verbal abuse or sexual abuse while in public spaces' (Whittle *et al.*, 2007, p. 53).

The NHS/Glasgow University 'Scottish Transgender Survey' of 2005 found that 'most (of the fifty-two transsexual) respondents had experienced verbal aggression ... most respondents had also experienced threats ... there were also many reports of physical aggression'. These 'were both physical and sexual, and ... committed by acquaintances, neighbours and strangers' (Wilson *et al.*, 2005, pp. 27–9).

Press for Change, in a report on transphobic hate crime in the European Union, the outcome of an online survey that received 2,669 responses, reported that four out of five (79%) respondents 'had experienced some form of harassment in public ranging from transphobic comments to physical or sexual abuse', leading the authors to suggest 'that trans people are three times more likely to experience a transphobic hate incident or crime than lesbians and gay men (are likely to experience) homophobic hate incidents or crimes'. In addition, a distinction between the experiences of MtF and FtM migrators was noted: '67% of trans women reported harassment compared to 57% of trans men' (Turner *et al.*, 2009, p. 1).

Transphobia also appears to be either becoming more widespread or is being more widely reported:

> some of the UK's biggest police forces have recorded a rise in transphobic hate crime, with victims subjected to assaults, verbal abuse and harassment in the street ... the Metropolitan Police saw offences against transgender people rise by 44% in 2014, with ninety-five crimes recorded, up from 66 (in 2013). Meanwhile Merseyside Police recorded thirty-two hate crimes, double the previous year (Mercer, 2014).

McNeil *et al.*'s recent survey for the STA, a UK-based online survey of mental health and transgender people in which 889 people took part, lists wide-ranging examples of apparently endemic transphobia:

> over 90% (of participants) had been told that trans people were not normal, over 80% had experienced silent harassment ... 50% had been sexually objectified or fetishised ... 38% had experienced sexual harassment, 13% had been sexually assaulted, and 6% had been raped ... over 37% had experienced physical threats or intimidation ... 19% had been hit or beaten up ... 25% had to move away from family or friends ... over 16% had experienced domestic abuse, and 14% had experienced police harassment (McNeil *et al.*, 2012, p. 88).

That transphobia might also be institutionalised and legally enforced was seen most recently in Russia, where transgender people have been banned from driving because 'transsexualism and transgenderism are now listed ... (alongside psychiatric disorders including schizophrenia and drug addiction) ... as examples of "mental disorders" that can make someone "unfit" to drive' (Rogers, 2015). While such treatment may seem unlikely to be copied within the UK, discrimination towards transgender people has nonetheless been evidenced within UK health services. Whittle *et al.* report that '21% of respondents' GPs did not want to help transgender people', and 'in 6% of cases … they actually refused to help them' (with transgender matters). In addition '17% of respondents had experience of a nurse or doctor … who did not approve of gender reassignment and hence refused services' (for non-transgender issues). 'Accessing healthcare was the … third highest sector where trans people encountered discrimination and inequality' and 'many local health authority funding refusals or refusals for care (were) from individual health service workers who expressed personal prejudice about gender dysphoria' (Whittle *et al.*, 2007, pp. 16, 43–5). The 2007 STA survey found that one in seven of respondents rated the quality of the service they received from their NHS General Practice as 'very' or 'extremely' poor. In addition, many respondents also commented on negative experiences of mental health services (Morton, 2008, pp. 11–18).

Underpinning attitudes to transgender

Hill and Willoughby, while carrying out pioneering work developing and validating a genderism and transphobia scale (GTS), found that 'the GTS was not simply measuring self-esteem, gender role orientation, or positive self-presentation strategies (but) was moderately associated with homophobia and gender role ideology' and that:

> the extent of negative attitudes toward gender non-conformists was somewhat surprising, considering the samples studied … were, by and large, well-educated members of a cosmopolitan city (Montreal) well-renowned for its liberal attitudes towards sexuality and gender issues (Hill and Willoughby, 2005, pp. 541–2).

Of relevance to this link with homophobia is Whittle *et al.*'s suggestion that 'much homophobic crime is actually transphobic, as it is a person's gender presentation which attracts attention … rather than … their sexual orientation' (Whittle *et al.*, 2007, p. 55). Connell explains how Butler not only regarded 'the medical diagnosis of "gender identity disorder" as a site of gender normativity' but how she also viewed 'anti-transgender violence as a sign of the ferocity with which heteronormativity is enforced' (Connell, 2012, p. 861).

Namaste suggests that the confusion and 'fusion of gender and sexuality has distinct implications for the problematic of violence' (Namaste, 2006, p. 588). She quotes Comstock's 1992 findings that 66% of gay men had been attacked when alone, while 44% of lesbian women had been attacked in pairs, but that 'these numbers are drastically reduced when men and women walk together: only 8% of women respondents were physically assaulted when they were with a man' and that this figure dropped to just 1% of male respondents when they were accompanied by women (Namaste, 2006, p. 589).

That transgender people may also be less at risk of antagonistic or transphobic behaviour in the company of a man or a woman might be anticipated from these findings. Although no figures regarding the effect of male or female companions on transphobic responses to MtF or FtM transgender people are currently available, it seems likely that either a male or female companion (or 'ally' – see Washington and Evans, 1991, p. 196 and the section on developing a more confident community presence in Chapter 7) might significantly reduce the likelihood of discriminatory behaviour from others. Conversely, the company of another transgender person, thereby perhaps increasing the visibility of each individual, may be *more* likely to lead to antagonistic or transphobic responses, though there appears to be an absence of research to support such speculation.

Mitchell and Howarth further explore the notion of underlying homophobic attitudes within their review of the transgender research literature, noting the 'discomfort that some people feel in terms of their sexual orientation when they cannot ascribe a fixed gender identity to a person' (Mitchell and Howarth, 2009, p. 35). Schilt and Westbrook concur with Mitchell and Howarth's findings in their own exploration of the links between gender, sexuality and transphobia, concluding: 'doing gender in a way that does not reflect biological sex can be perceived as a threat to heterosexuality', particularly in sexual (as opposed to social) situations (Schilt and Westbrook, 2009, p. 442).

Mitchell and Howarth also suggest that 'prejudice can be linked to sexism, the associated definition of rigid gender roles and behaviour linked to sex' (Mitchell and Howarth, 2009, p. 35). The possibility that transphobia may be elicited by sexism within very close family relationships is suggested by the findings of Whittle *et al.*, where higher levels of familial support were noted for transmen than for transwomen' (Whittle *et al.*, 2007, p. 69). This may be linked with lower levels of long-term success in integration or with passing for MtF trans people, for as Whittle notes 'in reality, despite all that medical technology can achieve, the majority of trans women cannot and will never pass' (although for those contemporary transitioners who are able to avoid the permanent effects of puberty by the use of puberty blockers, the likelihood of successful passing after transition may be much increased). In relation to FtM people, Whittle adds that, 'although "passing" might appear at first glance easily achieved, the limitations of gender reassignment mean that they will never be able to form a sexual relationship without having to disclose their past' (Whittle, 2000, pp. 49–50).

In an extraordinary piece of research, Westbrook collected newspaper data on a total of 232 murders in the United States of (predominantly MtF) transgender people 'doing gender so as to possibly be seen as a gender other than the one they were assigned at birth'. Her findings indicated that more than a half (56%) of reports spoke of perpetrators being deceived by the victim, within a sexual context (Schilt and Westbrook, 2009, pp. 445–6). However, direct reference to the list of people commemorated at the Transgender Day of Remembrance (GLAAD, 2014) very often does not give enough information to be clear as to the reason for each murder. Incidentally, even a cursory perusal of this website indicates that such deaths are predominantly reported from within North and South America (particularly the USA, Brazil and Mexico). Murders of transgender people within European countries are recorded in limited numbers, the most numerous apparently being perpetrated in Turkey.

That racism may also contribute to the likelihood of murder is suggested by a *Guardian* report of the killing of a black transgender nurse in Mississippi in July 2016, the second such murder of a black transgender woman in less than three weeks in the USA and the fifteenth homicide of a transgender person within a seven-month period. The senior manager of National Research and Policy at the National Coalition of Anti-Violence Projects (NCAVP) commented that 'the violence that transgender women of colour face is rooted in racism, misogyny, homophobia and transphobia' (*The Guardian*, 2016b).

Schilt and Westbrook's study of the 'repatriation' of FtM individuals within the workplace suggested that:

heterosexual women ... police the boundaries of who can be counted as a man – in sexualised situations, transmen's masculinity is simultaneously reinforced – as men frame them as heterosexual men – and challenged – as women position them as homosexual women' (Schilt and Westbrook, 2009, pp. 442, 445, 447).

Again, this indicates a conflation of sex, gender and sexuality. Whether this position is reversed for MtF individuals (i.e. that men are more likely to view trans women as gay men, and women are more likely to accept them as heterosexual women) would be the basis for valuable further research.

Discrimination and partner relationships

That marriages or relationships falter or break up when a transgender person comes out, either to their partner or on a wider scale, is suggested by Jeffreys, who notes that 'female partners of men who transgender ... often find it impossible to accept that their husbands have become women' and find it difficult to use pronouns for them that they understand to be specific to their own experience as women (Jeffreys, 2014, p. 9). Benvenuto, for example, refers only to 'he' and 'him' throughout her 294-page account of her (and her children's) experience of her husband's/their father's transition, and beyond, because 'even now I can't think, speak, or write about this' (Benvenuto, 2012, pp. 193).

Evidence of problematic attitudes within the close relationships of transgender people was put forward by the Scottish LGBT Domestic Abuse project, which identified eight domestic behaviours that it termed transphobic. These included being stopped from expressing one's gender identity through appearance and/or through use of name and pronouns, being stopped from sharing information with others about one's trans background or identity, or being made to feel shame, guilt or wrong about one's trans background or identity. Some 73% of forty-five respondents said that their partner or ex-partner had carried out at least one of these eight behaviours (Roch et al., 2010, p. 15).

It seems reasonable to infer from these findings that relationship difficulties may arise when a partner comes out or undertakes gender

reassignment/confirmation. Whether the use of the term 'transphobic' is appropriate to describe such a response as not using the preferred pronoun is perhaps only understandable within each partnership
dynamic: Ladin suggests that 'non-supportive partners are portrayed
as problems to be coped with, rather than as suffering individuals in
their own right' (Ladin, 2012, p. 24), highlighting the need for greater
understanding of the effects of transition on close family members.

However, Jeffreys goes further than simply defending accusations
of transphobia against partners, citing what she describes as 'psychological violence' by transgender husbands who 'go beyond a lack of
empathy with their partners suffering and become more abusive' (Jeffreys, 2014, p. 86). She also refers to 'abusive relationships' by lesbian
partners, evidence for which is cited within a study by Brown (2007),
where partners (of transitioning individuals) reported manipulation,
emotional and verbal abuse, name calling and demeaning put-downs
(Jeffreys, 2014, pp. 115).

Jeffreys goes on to note that 'no research has specifically examined
this problem' so it is difficult to speculate on the degree to which partners of MtF or FtM transgender people do themselves feel isolated,
unsupported, distressed, helpless, and/or abused, but clearly such con-
siderations need to be taken into account in the provision of social care
support to partners and families of transgender people (see Chapter
6), while also recognising that some transgender people retain their
long-term relationships with partners prior to and following gender
reassignment/confirmation, within apparently continuing mutually
caring and supportive roles. So, for example, while the pair of books by
Ladin and Benvenuto, published in 2012, describe two quite different
perspectives on the fragmentation of the same marriage during and following transition, Jan Morris, whose transition in the 1970s is referred
to several times within this book, remarried her former wife within a
civil union, in 2008, almost sixty years after their original marriage,
and some thirty years post-transition, having continued to live together
throughout the intervening period (BBC News Channel, 2008).

Transgender erasure
The apparent limited awareness by social care organisations of the
needs of transgender people within the Scottish 2015 study (Norman,

2015a, pp. 427–9) appears to reflect Namaste's observation that: 'if we actually do empirical research on some of the matters most pressing for transsexuals ... we discover that (they) are quite literally shut out and excluded from the institutional world' (Namaste, 2011, p. 3). Bauer *et al.* suggest, in recognising that 'trans people represent one of the most marginalised groups in our society', that in relation to health services 'care providers lack of preparation for working with trans patients stems in part from inaccurate current estimates of the size of trans populations'. The absence of knowledge about transgender populations and transgender need evidenced in Scottish local authorities within the Scottish 2015 study (Norman, 2015a, p. 178) appears to fall into what Bauer *et al.* call 'informational erasure', which 'encompasses both a lack of knowledge regarding trans people and trans issues and the assumption that such knowledge does not exist' (Bauer *et al.*, 2009, pp. 349, 352, 354).

In relation to the Scottish 2015 study there was often a disarming honesty in the degree to which some statutory representatives admitted to such a lack of knowledge and offered their constructive suggestions to try to address gaps in both knowledge and services: for example, the notion of smaller local authorities working together to meet the needs of local transgender people (Norman, 2015a, p. 184). Using figures from two respected sources regarding the likely incidence of transgender people provides increasingly accurate estimates of the numbers of transsexual individuals (see the section on incidence and levels of transgender need in Chapter 2). These relatively small levels do indeed support the notion of local councils and voluntary services co-working to provide dedicated services and, as appropriate, to better develop guidance and policies on transgender accessibility to local generic services.

Bauer *et al.* go on to suggest that 'the perception that trans-people are rare reinforces an erasure of trans communities and the continuing treatment of trans people as isolated cases (leading to their) cumulative invisibility' (Bauer *et al.*, 2009, p. 354). Recognising that creative service development across local authorities – for example, by sharing responsibility for the provision of transgender group support – can make a significant difference to the lives of transgender people in a local area might help to counterbalance the effects of such erasure and invisibility.

Feminism and transgender women

A number of female academic feminists have taken an extremely critical view of (mainly MtF) transgender people and transsexuals. As Connell notes in her review of transsexual women and feminist thought:

> transsexual women are a small group who have been subject to fierce and extended scrutiny … (which) … includes a feminist literature that exposes a troubled and often antagonistic relationship between feminism and transsexual women.

For example, 'Daly (1978) attacked transsexuality as a "necrophilic invasion" of women's bodies and spirits' (Connell, 2012, pp. 857, 860), while Raymond's (1980) book *The Transsexual Empire* was viewed by Stryker and Whittle as the forerunner of a 'politically progressive ethical condemnation of transsexualism'. They went on to suggest that, although Raymond's book 'did not invent anti-transsexual prejudice … it did more to justify and perpetuate it than any book ever written' (Stryker and Whittle, 2006, p. 131).

Whittle suggests that 'Raymond's thesis … discredited for a long time any academic voice that … (the transgender community) … might have, in particular with feminist theorists' (Whittle, 1996, p. 207). The consequences of such widespread prejudice are eloquently expressed by Ladin, who recounts:

> since transition, I had avoided women-only events as scrupulously as I had when I was a man. Janice Raymond wasn't the only woman who didn't accept the validity of male-to-female transition; at a Sukkot gathering of queer congregants at my local synagogue, one lesbian told me frankly that, after her history of abuse by men, she felt violated when she found transwomen in women-only spaces (Ladin, 2012, p. 234).

Jeffreys' recent publication, which is described on its cover as a 'provocative and controversial book … (which) … offers a feminist perspective on the ideology and practice of transgenderism, which the author sees as harmful' (Jeffreys, 2014) and which contains praise by Raymond as a book of 'exceptional courage, clarity and scholarship (which) interrogates the dogma of transgenderism', suggests that such discussions and arguments are far from resolved. Stryker and Whittle summarise Raymond's views, which suggest that transwomen:

> remain deviant men ... (using) ... the appropriated appearance of the female body to invade women's spaces ... in order to exercise male dominance and aggression ... an undesired penetration ... tantamount to rape (so) that all MtF transsexuals are by definition rapists (Stryker and Whittle, 2006, p.131).

Raymond's views are extraordinary in their lack of insight into transgender people's motivation to transition. Such views might simply be dismissed as unreasonable if they were not still 'uncritically accepted by some on the cultural left ... as a paragon of feminist criticism of medical-scientific practices' (Stryker and Whittle, 2006, p. 131).

Almost forty years after *The Transsexual Empire* in 1979, the uncompromising criticism of transwomen within Jeffreys' book suggests that such views still pervade some feminist thinking. It might be hypothesised that 'equity feminists' and 'gender feminists' (a distinction taken from Hoff Sommers, 1994) might differ in their degree of criticism and acceptance of transgender people, particularly as a deeper awareness of the nature of gender transition becomes more widely understood.

Life histories and core values
Germaine Greer (1999) too has commented on MtF transgender people with an approach that suggests little progress within at least some feminist, intellectual and/or academic communities: Greer shows no empathy or understanding for MtF individuals when she writes that 'when a man decides to spend his life impersonating his mother (like Norman Bates in Psycho) ... his intentions are no more honourable than any female impersonator's ... when he forces his way into the few private spaces women may enjoy and shouts down their objections, and bombards the women who will not accept him with threats and hate mail, he does as rapists have always done' (Greer 1999, p. 74).

In contrast, the position of the FtM transsexual man is discussed by Jeffreys, who suggests that 'the transgendering of women is an antidote to feminism because it is a way in which individual women can raise their status by joining the caste of men' (Jeffreys, 2014, p. 101). It may, somewhat ironically, be the case that transgender men largely escape criticism by feminists in academic writing or the media because, as Schilt and Westbrook suggest, although 'men frame them

as heterosexual men … women position them as homosexual women'
(Schilt and Westbrook, 2009, pp. 442, 445, 447).

Both Greer and Raymond recognise a dilemma faced by many transsexual people within society – that they lack a 'history' in their preferred gender role (and indeed that they bring with them, consciously
or unconsciously, their 'history' in their original gender role). It seems
likely that such limited social and cultural experiences may result in
some difficulty in adapting to, and feeling at ease within, the binary
gender role to which one transitions, despite a lifetime of wishing for
such a transition, or feeling 'trapped' within the wrong body.

The notion of 'history' also plays a major role in 'passing' at a level
beyond that of appearance and behaviour. It seems that some transsexuals create a history at transition which fits with their new role, seeking
to start their lives again in a new location with a 'clean sheet' and with
stories from a fictional 'boyhood' or 'girlhood' to recount, which fit
with their post-transition selves and which may provide another level of
protection against transphobia and hate crime. Meyerowitz notes that,
from the earliest days of more widespread gender reassignment, 'Benjamin and others urged post-operative patients to hide, and even to lie
about, their past lives as the other sex' (Meyerowitz, 2006, p. 382). For
some transgender people, though, the notion of making up a childhood,
adolescent and adult history to suit their new gender role is too close
to being an extension of the 'living a lie' that was part of the chronic
difficulty of living in their original gender role. Goffman, in a broader
discussion of stigma, acknowledges the intrinsic pervasive nature of the
dilemma of 'the management of undisclosed discrediting information,
about self … in brief, "passing" ' through which an individual with a
stigmatising condition must decide 'to display or not to display; to tell
or not to tell; to let on or not to let on; to lie or not to lie; and in each
case, to whom, how, when and where' (Goffman, 1968, pp. 57–8).

One potential problem with constructing such an artificial history is
that, if such a transsexual is found out, the notion that they might be now
perceived as someone who has performed a deception might undermine
at least in part the credibility that they have gained as an individual within
their community. It may even be possible that this aspect of some transsexuals' behaviour might be considered as a possible contributory factor to
prejudice and rejection within their community, and to the emergence and

fuelling of transphobia. It is, however, worth bearing in mind that, according to the Beyond Barriers report on LGBT people in Scotland, only 80% of LGB people were open about their sexuality with their family, while 95% were open about this with their friends, but this figure dropped to approximately 66% with their GP or employer, 75% with work colleagues, just over 50% with teachers and lecturers and just under 50% with a faith group (Morgan and Bell, 2003). Caution regarding the sharing of intimately personal information is not just the prerogative of transgender people in a less than open-minded society.

The notion of a lack of history is not, however, simply a matter of adjusting to or passing within gender-divided social conventions. If, for example, one has lived through the formative gendered years of childhood, adolescence and early adulthood in a male role before transitioning to a female role, this may result in a significantly altered status within society, which may affect self-esteem and self-perception, making adaptation to a post-transition role more difficult. Similarly, someone who began life living as a girl or woman who then transitions may initially at least feel somewhat uncomfortable by the new status that he gradually acquires alongside his acceptance as a man, bringing into clearer focus the differences in opportunity which were available to him previously as a woman.

The key issue of gender-based 'core values', supposedly acquired and assimilated during the period of time which was spent in one's original gender role, also needs to be researched. It might be argued that the nature of such values (if indeed such core values can be identified and subsequently isolated from the gender roles which might be expected to underpin them) affects and is affected by relationships with others before and after transition. It may be that some transgender people feel that they have never identified with core values associated with their original gender role or that they reconsidered their original values in the light of their experiences within the gender role they adopted. Khosla, for example, in a remarkable exploration of his own attitude to rape, explains his position from both his original (female) role, and from that of the male status he has now adopted. He also shows self-awareness at how his changing appearance affects eye contact and body movements in women, when walking at night or in an isolated area (Khosla, 2006, p. 132).

It may be that if such issues as personal or core values are to be resolved at an individual level, and understood at a wider level, the role and importance of pre-transition personal history and of post-transition adaptation of behaviour and values may need to be acknowledged to a greater extent than is currently apparent. Similarly there is a paucity of information about the degree to which gender transition results in alterations to lifestyles, leisure interests and activities, and to the nature and extent of personal relationships and friendships within social circles. Each of these factors will play a role in the degree of mental well-being experienced following transition by both MtF and FtM transgender people, and this topic forms the basis for the next chapter of this book.

CHAPTER 5

Physical and Mental Health Issues

Introduction

Bockting *et al.* stress the wide-ranging, holistic nature of mental health when they suggest that it:

> is intrinsically connected to cultural, physical, sexual, psychosocial and spiritual aspects of health ... (and that) ... for individuals seeking help relating to gender concerns, the clinician must be knowledgeable about gender and sexual identity development, transgender 'coming out', cross-dressing, gender dysphoria, gender transition and the common concerns and reactions of loved ones (Bockting *et al.*, 2006, pp. 1–2).

They note the intense pressures that may affect 'many transgender individuals (for whom) the daily trials of living in a transphobic society constitutes ongoing trauma', commenting that some transgender individuals 'described life as a daily humiliation' (Bockting *et al.*, 2006, p. 35). This chapter explores studies into mental health issues prior to and following transition, including long term 'follow-up' reviews.

Mental health and transgender

Lawrence found that 'some transgender persons ... appear to have an elevated prevalence of co-existing mental health problems' (Lawrence, 2007, p. 473), while Mind, the mental health charity, explains on its website that 'the available evidence suggests that LGBT people have a higher risk of experiencing suicidal feelings, self-harm, drug or alcohol misuse and mental health problems such as depression and anxiety' (Mind, 2013). Greenwood and Gruskin note 'high levels of daily stress due to stigma ... discrimination ... and transphobia for ... transgenders' (*sic*) while also noting 'high rates of smoking ... and drinking' (Greenwood and Gruskin, 2007, pp. 566–72).

The NHS/Glasgow University survey found that levels of self-harm in transgender respondents 'far-exceeded expected population norms' (Wilson *et al.*, 2005, p. 28). In a breakdown of incidence within MtF and FtM individuals they found that, among:

> the MtF respondents, eighteen of thirty-nine had self-harmed, most commonly by taking overdoses of pills. Seven were currently self-harming (i.e. within the past year), most commonly by scratching, hitting or burning. A similarly high proportion, seven of thirteen of the FtM respondents, had self-harmed, most commonly by cutting or scratching (Wilson *et al.*, 2005, p. 16).

McNeil *et al.* found that 52% of participants had self-harmed in the past, with more than one in ten (11%) currently self-harming (McNeil *et al.*, 2012, p. 88). Lastly, Kennedy and Hellen note that transgender children 'achieve well below their abilities at school ... and are more likely to self-harm or attempt suicide and are more likely to suffer from mental health issues in early adulthood', which may lead to 'substantial underachievement in all areas of their lives' (Kennedy and Hellen, 2010, pp. 25, 40).

Kenagy, in a study of 182 transgender individuals in Philadelphia in 1997, found that 30% had attempted suicide (Kenagy, 2005, p. 19). Similarly, Morrow, in a discussion of social work practice with LGBT adolescents, indicated that 'an alarming 30% to 40% of GLBT (*sic*) youth have attempted suicide ... in comparison to a suicide rate of 8% to 13% for presumed heterosexual youth' (Morrow, 2004, p. 95). McNeil *et al.* found that 84% of participants had thought about ending their lives at some point, with more than one in four (27%) having had these thoughts in *the week* previous to completing the survey and almost two-thirds (63%) during the year prior to the survey. However, 'suicidal ideation and actual attempts reduced after transition, with 63% thinking about or attempting suicide more before they transitioned and only 3% thinking about or attempting suicide more post-transition' (McNeil *et al.*, 2012, p. 89).

Within the Scottish 2015 study, eighteen (38%) of forty-seven respondents said that they had a mental health condition that had lasted or was expected to last at least twelve months (with one other also suffering from depression), while fifteen respondents (32%) stated that they had a 'long-term illness, disease or condition'. Ten respondents (21%) reported suffering from a range of physical conditions (Norman, 2015a, p. 284). These are much higher figures than those of the Scottish Household Survey, which indicated a national average of 5% who are 'permanently sick or disabled' (Scottish Government, 2013, Section 5).

Cross-tabulation indicated that of the twenty-seven respondents who had transitioned to, and were currently living in their preferred gender role, five of those in a male gender role (four of whom were in the age group 16–25), seven in a female gender role (five of whom were in the age group 46–55), and five in a transgender role said that they had a mental health condition (seventeen in total). These findings suggest potential associations between age, gender identity and mental health linked with imminent, ongoing or recently completed transition (Norman, 2015a, pp. 284–6).

The unexpectedly high number of respondents who described themselves as having a mental health condition that had lasted or was expected to last at least twelve months suggests that McNeil's finding of '63% thinking about or attempting suicide … before they transitioned' (McNeil *et al.*, 2012, p. 89) may indeed have relevance to the pre-transition respondents of this research, and that this vulnerability may extend into the post-transition period too: 'I suffer from depression and anxiety especially in public places due to being verbally and physically abused for being transgender' (Norman, 2015a, p. 276).

This latter comment from one of the transitioned MtF survey respondents suggests that one of the main reasons why transgender people have a higher risk of experiencing suicidal feelings and mental health problems may be the effect of persistent stress, linked with transphobia, which, when added to the difficulties of understanding one's own gender and resolving transition issues, may make life at times seem unbearable. Whittle *et al.* evidenced early encounters with anti-transgender attitudes when they observed that almost two-thirds of young trans-men and almost a half of young trans-women experienced harassment or bullying at school, not just from their fellow pupils, but also from school staff, including teachers. That a transgender person's GP may be unsympathetic may also be a significant contributory factor to low self-esteem, and rejection by one's family may also have a very detrimental effect (Whittle *et al.*, 2007, pp. 16, 17).

It is, therefore, reassuring to find that of the forty-two survey respondents within the Scottish 2015 study, thirty (71%) said that their day-to-day activities were not limited because of a mental health problem linked with being transgender. However, eight people stated that their day-to-day activities were restricted a lot, while four others said that they were confined a little because of such a problem – almost 30% of respondents in total (Table 5.1; Norman, 2015a, p. 276).

Table 5.1: Limitations to day-to-day activities because of a mental health problem or disability linked with being transgender which has lasted, or is expected to last, at least twelve months (Survey one: n = 47).

Degree of limitation by mental health problem or disability linked with being transgender	Number of respondents	Percentage of respondents
My day-to-day activities are limited a lot by a mental health problem or disability linked with being transgender	8	19
My day-to-day activities are limited a little by a mental health problem or disability linked with being transgender	4	10
My day-to-day activities are not limited by a mental health problem or disability linked with being transgender	30	71
Total	42	100

Mental health pre- and post-transition

The NHS/Glasgow University survey found that 'the vast majority of respondents reported major psychological distress before transition' but that there was a significant difference following the transition process, evidenced by 'scores on the mental health scales (which suggested) that operative intervention improved mental health' with a noticeable difference in well-being following the transition process (Wilson *et al.*, 2005, pp. 28–9). Indeed, McNeil *et al.* found that '45% of participants had used mental health services more before transition, 18% more during, and 0% more … post transition' (McNeil *et al.*, 2012, p. 87). However, what is not clear is the time period after transition for each respondent to these surveys (although twenty-six of the thirty-seven MtF participants of the Glasgow survey had completed real-life experience as females, for a mean of two years (Wilson *et al.*, 2005, p. 16).

It is not known whether there is a 'honeymoon' period after transition when the relief that appears to result from the process is at its most intense, and whether this fades somewhat as the reality of living in a less than accepting world, and a greater awareness of visibility and difficulties in passing intrude into the sense of conflict resolution. Longer-term studies are needed to clarify fluctuations in life satisfaction over time, and some of these are reviewed in the section on Follow-up studies below.

The STA survey of 2012 found that '70% of participants were more satisfied with their lives since transitioning and only 2% were less satisfied', for reasons linked with 'poor surgical outcome, loss of family, friends and employment, everyday experiences of transphobia and non-trans-related reasons'. However, this same survey also indicated that:

> 70% of respondents felt that they had lost or missed out on something as a result of being trans, transitioning or expressing their gender identity (including) jobs and a career, money, reproduction, home, childhood and youth, sports and leisure opportunities, equality and respect, family life, relationships and dating, happiness, friendships, intimacy, social life, personal development, education and qualifications.

It is not clear how such an extensive sense of loss, over so many life experiences, is addressed or reconciled by each transgender individual who undertakes transition. In summary, 78% of participants 'reported that recognising their gender identity or transitioning had improved their quality of life, compared to 9% who thought it had got worse' (n = 499) (McNeil *et al.*, 2012, pp. 82, 87–9).

These findings are counter-balanced by the 81% of participants who, as a result of being trans, transitioning or expressing their gender identity, felt that they had gained:

> confidence, new friends, improved/better quality relationships, community and a sense of belonging, self-expression and acceptance, knowledge and insight, happiness and contentment, resilience, and a future.

While '53% had no regrets (and) 34% had minimal regrets', almost one in eleven '(9%) had significant regrets ... in terms of social changes that they had made in relation to being trans'. The most commonly recorded regrets were 'not having the body that they wanted from birth, not transitioning sooner/earlier (problems with surgery and) losing friends and family':

> Most worried that other people would find their bodies unattractive (81%) or that few people would want to have sex with them (79%) (while) 58% were also worried about their physical safety in relation to having sex.

Many participants, following transition, also noted changes in their sex lives: 'while 38% indicated that this had improved, 20% felt that their sex life had worsened following transition' (McNeil *et al.*, 2012, pp. 89–90).

Follow-up studies and reviews

A study by Pfäfflin and Junge, one of the most extensive reviews in the literature, considered thirty years of follow-up studies in the English and German language, consisting of almost eighty papers and reviews 'of approximately two thousand persons who have undergone sex reassignment surgery' (Pfäfflin and Junge, 1998, p. 1). Many of these reviews were at a period of approximately two to three years after surgery, but 'fourteen publications about women and nine about men, and two that do not differentiate by gender reported a follow up period of at least five years since "the surgery"' (Pfäfflin and Junge, 1998, p. 27), which is an important balance to what might otherwise be a somewhat limited review of the 'honeymoon period' after transition.

The main conclusion of the Pfäfflin and Junge review was that:

> gender reassigning treatments are effective. Positive ... desired ... effects overweigh continuously ... negative or non-desired effects (although) the results with (FtM people) are on average somewhat more favourable than those with (MtF people).

Subjective satisfaction results ranged within a spectrum of 71% to 87% for MtF people, and from 89% to 97% for FtM people (Pfäfflin and Junge, 1998, pp. 39–40). They also conclude that MtF patients were more likely to suffer social isolation, while FtM patients were more able to maintain stable and satisfactory partnerships (Pfäfflin and Junge, 1998, p. 44). Pfäfflin and Junge also note that 'dependency on social welfare (was) predominant amongst (MtF) patients' (Pfäfflin and Junge, 1998, pp. 54–5).

De Cuypere *et al.* reviewed thirty-five MtF and twenty-seven FtM transsexuals who had undergone SRS between 1986 and 2001 in Ghent. They indicated that while:

> the subjects proclaimed an overall positive change in their family and social life (and) none of them showed regrets about the SRS ... a homosexual orientation (at referral), a younger age when applying for SRS and an attractive physical appearance were positive prognostic factors (De Cuypere *et al.*, 2006, pp. 126–7).

A further study of 141 Dutch transsexuals (36 FtM people and 105 MtF people) by Kuiper and Cohen-Kettenis concludes that 'there is no reason to doubt the therapeutic effect of sex reassignment surgery' (Kuiper and Cohen-Kettenis, 1988, p. 439). They did, however, note that only about two-thirds of the sample (ninety-two individuals, 65.2%) indicated that they felt happy or very happy, while thirty-three (23.4%) said that they were moderately happy, and more than ten (sixteen, 11.3%) described themselves as unhappy or very unhappy. When Kuiper and Cohen-Kettenis scrutinised these results and analysed what patients meant by happiness, they reported:

> feeling more free, experiencing more inner calm, being relieved and glad that desire and reality had become one (with) positive references to the SRS. However, one factor in particular was related to 'experienced happiness': 'having a steady partner'.

Conversely, 'feeling unhappy usually correlated with a sense of loneliness'. Kuiper and Cohen-Kettenis conclude from this that the 'absence or termination of a steady relationship is of decisive significance in this respect for many persons' (Kuiper and Cohen-Kettenis, 1988, p. 445).

Kuiper and Cohen-Kettenis also explored the notion of regret by asking if patients 'ever have doubts about your sense of being a man (or woman)'. Some 136 of the 141 patients 'reported no or hardly any doubts about their own gender identity': just one FtM person and three MtF people felt occasional doubts (Kuiper and Cohen-Kettenis, 1988, p. 448). However, although the majority of respondents were satisfied with their 'own behaviour as a man (FtM) or a woman (MtF)', eight MtF people felt either dissatisfied (seven) or very dissatisfied (one) with this aspect of their identity. This outcome may be partially explained by responses to the question 'how well do you in your opinion pass as a member of the newly assumed gender?' Kuiper and Cohen-Kettenis report that 'virtually all FtMs and almost 80% of the MtFs describe integration as good or very good by their own standards' (Kuiper and Cohen-Kettenis, 1988, p. 446). They explain that 'most of the problems reported ... can be divided into two categories: (i) physical problems like a too low-pitched voice ... no penis' etc. and 'problems in overt management of their transsexual background in relation to a new partner, colleagues, or parents-in-law' (Kuiper and Cohen-Kettenis, 1988, pp. 446–7).

In addition, Kuiper and Cohen-Kettenis note that 'lack of understanding and discrimination are mentioned by six FtMs (of thirty-six) and seventeen MtFs (of 105)' and that 'strikingly, the FtMs mention only *lack of understanding*, whereas the MtFs emphasize *discrimination*' (Kuiper and Cohen-Kettenis, 1988, p. 447, italics added). They also found that:

> one of the FtMs attempted suicide, about two years after starting treatment (but that) fifteen of the MtFs attempted suicide, mostly within two to five years of starting therapy. Ten were motivated in their attempt by psychosocial problems and the associated feelings of loneliness and depression.

They also note that three MtF people (but no FtM) committed suicide in the last ten years of the survey (Kuiper and Cohen-Kettenis, 1988, p. 451).

Kuiper and Cohen-Kettenis also found a correlation between subjective well-being and ten variables: employment; acceptance by family; partnership; sense of loneliness; satisfaction with relations in general; gender role behaviour; integration of new gender role in day-to-day life; general satisfaction with sex life; certainty about one's own gender identity; and suicidal attempts' (Kuiper and Cohen-Kettenis, 1988, p. 452). It seems that these factors may additively affect the overall satisfaction outcomes of transition, suggesting the possibility that the long-term prognosis for transitioned transgender people does not consistently support the notion that transition will result in less mental health issues across all migrators. Indeed, Dhejne *et al.*, in a 'long-term follow up of (324) transsexual persons undergoing sex assignment surgery' in Sweden, found 'substantially higher rates of overall mortality, death from cardio-vascular disease and suicide, suicide attempts, and psychiatric hospitalisations in sex-reassigned transsexual individuals compared to a healthy control population' (Dhejne *et al.*, 2011, p. 7).

Kuiper and Cohen-Kettenis are particularly explicit in their recognition of the need for social support or 'psychosocial guidance in addition to medical guidance' for issues other than those directly related to gender dysphoria. They explain that:

> many transsexuals undergoing SRS (especially MtFs) lose their jobs, their relationships with (part of) their families, their partners (if any) and children, and their friends. Many are forced or feel forced to move away from their familiar environment ... social adaptation is not always easy. Not infrequently, significant others are lost, social isolation ensues and a sense of existential loneliness is experienced. It is understandable that such a situation saps the emotional strength of the person. Although the new situation appears to reduce the gender problems experienced, the loss situations unfortunately mar the process of sex reassignment in many cases (Kuiper and Cohen-Kettenis, 1988, p. 455).

Support with long-term physical or mental ill health etc.

Just under a half (twenty-one of forty-seven) participants in the Scottish 2015 survey responded to a question about sources of support with long-term ill health etc., summarised in Table 5.2.

GPs were rated as of the highest importance as a source of advice and support regarding long-term physical or mental ill health, disability or problems related to old age, by nine of a total of twenty-one respondents, with mainly positive ratings indicated by both those who had transitioned to a male or a female gender role. Counsellors or psychiatrists also received mainly positive ratings by both those in a male or female gender role.

Table 5.2: The importance of sources of advice or support for long-term ill health, disability or problems related to old age
(Survey one: n = 47: 21 respondents).

Key: Importance of sources of advice and support regarding physical or mental ill health, disability or old age
(1 = highest importance, 11 = least importance).

Source/Importance of Advice or Support for long-term ill health, disability or problems related to old age	1	2	3	4	5	6	7	8	9	10	11
a. Close Friends	3	5	3	0	1	0	0	0	0	2	5
b. Family Members	7	1	0	0	1	0	0	0	1	0	7
c. Colleagues at Work/Line Manager	0	1	1	0	1	0	0	0	1	0	10
d. Transgender Support Group	3	0	2	2	1	2	0	1	1	0	3
e. General Practitioner	9	1	1	0	0	2	1	0	0	1	3
f. Gender Specialist at G.I.C.	0	3	0	0	0	2	0	1	1	0	7
g. Speech Therapist	1	0	0	0	1	0	1	0	0	0	8
h. Health Visitor or District Nurse	0	0	0	0	0	0	1	0	1	0	10
i. Counsellor or Psychiatrist	7	3	1	0	1	0	1	1	1	0	3
j. Social Worker	1	0	1	0	0	1	0	1	0	1	7
k. Carer/PersonalAssistant/SupportWorker	1	1	0	1	0	0	0	1	0	0	9

A	B	C	D	E	F
16>	11–15	6–10	16>	11–15	6–10

For full explanation of typographic coding, please see table 1.1 on p. 13.

A three-way cross-tabulation indicated that each of the three respondents in a current male gender role and with a male gender identity rated close friends in the three highest categories for support with long-term health issues. Of the nine respondents in a current female gender role and with a female gender identity only four considered close friends as falling into the three highest categories, with the remaining respondents placing them in the three lowest categories.

Perhaps surprisingly, given the earlier findings noted regarding support differences to MtF and FtM individuals, levels of family support with long-term health issues, though relatively low, were similarly rated by those in both a male and female gender role. Social and care workers received very low ratings of importance, in general (Norman, 2015a, p. 285).

Mental health support and treatment

A survey by the STA found that many respondents commented on negative experiences of mental health services, leading to the conclusion that a 'lack of understanding and knowledge about transgender issues by general psychiatrists often results in transgender people being given inappropriate treatment which fails to assist them with their gender dysphoria' (Morton, 2008, pp. 11–18). Indeed, the NHS/Glasgow University study found that 'the single most important health issue (for transgender people) is the lack of appropriate mental health services for trans-people' (Wilson *et al.*, 2005, pp. 28–9).

The value of psychotherapeutic treatment for transsexuality has been seriously questioned, because, as Morris explained: 'patients with gender disorders do not want therapy ... they want surgery'. Nonetheless, he goes on to argue that 'gender patients both require and deserve psychotherapeutic input in order to be able to clarify their motivations for seeking gender reassignment treatment' (Morris, in Barrett, 2007, pp. 91, 100). It might also be added that transgender people considering transition should be made aware of the outcomes found in long-term follow-up studies, prior to making what is likely to be an irreversible decision with such profound, life-changing consequences.

Whittle has argued that 'the medical discourse surrounding transgendered behaviour which labels them (*sic*) mentally ill (is one of) several big obstacles to be overcome' (Whittle, 2000, p. 45). Despite many transgender people believing that the condition of being transgender should not be regarded as a disease, it was still included, at the point of this book going to press, within 'the ICD-10 (the International Classification of Diseases) (where it was defined) as a desire to live and be accepted as a member of the opposite sex, usually accompanied by a sense of discomfort with one's anatomical sex' (Barrett, 2007, p. 17). Whittle noted that the American Psychiatric Association's 'Diagnostic and statistical manual of mental disorders' (DSM-3) 'removed homosexuality from the list of psychosexual disorders, while at the same time it added transsexuality' (Whittle, 1996, p. 197). However, the 2013 version (DSM-5) noted that having a transgender or gender non-conforming identity will no longer be classified as a mental disorder. Instead, the notion of gender identity disorder is replaced by gender dysphoria whose critical diagnostic feature is '*clinically significant distress* associated with the condition' (American Psychiatric Association, 2013, italic added).

Increasing rejection of medical diagnoses of transgender conditions as disorders of personality and behaviour within ICD-10 has resulted in pressure to amend the next ICD edition accordingly, in 2017. However, McNeil *et al.*'s survey found that 29% of the respondents felt that their gender identity was not validated as genuine within mental health services, instead being perceived as a symptom of mental ill health ... 17% were also told that their mental health issues were because they were trans' (when they themselves saw them as a separate issue) (McNeil *et al.*, 2012, p. 87).

Lastly, some transgender respondents appeared to feel that problems with physical or mental health were either viewed through a 'transgender' perspective by their GP, or that their transgender status might affect the treatment or support they might receive (Norman, 2015a, p. 288).

> **Luke:** 'I have had illnesses that anyone could get, yet it has been turned into a massive fiasco because I am transgender and find accessing healthcare very difficult. Someone to help balance out what I should and shouldn't be talking to my doctor about would be helpful, because for the most part I don't, other than to refill prescriptions. And someone to reassure (me) that no, I am not unwell because I am transgender' (Norman, 2015a, p. 289).

It was also suggested by one interviewee within the Scottish 2015 study that living within a small town/rural community, without the anonymity of a larger city, and with limited access to a transgender support group or to the nearest GIC, might place additional stress on a transgender person:

> **Ciaran:** 'I live in a small town and as you can imagine everyone knows everyone else's business so it didn't take long before I was verbally abused for being a 'freak' and even assaulted in public more than once. I would like to move away to a place where nobody knows me and I can leave the house without having panic attacks, but my family are here (the ones that haven't disowned me) and my angel of a fiancée/her family' (Norman, 2015a, p. 279).

The notion of such a 'small town mentality' within smaller communities was extended to the local mental health services on offer by another interviewee:

> **Lucy:** 'The trouble with local services in an area like this is that (they are) staffed by folk who come from the area, which is very regressive for LGBT people. We have a small population and a resultant small local mental health team who to a great degree reflect the inherent local prejudices' (Norman, 2015a, p. 279).

One potential consequence of such 'inherent local prejudices' may be withdrawal and exclusion from a wide range of social contacts. Within the Scottish 2015 study eleven of twenty-seven respondents said that they would greatly value advice, information and support to help address social isolation linked with being transgender. When cross-tabulated with biological sex, seven of twelve biological males and two of ten biological females said that they would value this information and support greatly. Including those who would value such support a little brought these numbers up to sixteen of the twenty-seven transgender individuals, suggesting that social isolation may be a very significant contributor to mental health issues associated with being transgender (Norman, 2015a, pp. 280–1). Indeed, it is possible that for some individuals the negative effects of social isolation may be as damaging and pervasive as those of transphobia, leading to the increasing reclusivity of the transgender person:

> **Ciaran:** 'I would love to be out working again but the anxiety I feel about even leaving the house some days overwhelms me' (Norman, 2015a, p. 299).

Sixteen of the twenty-seven respondents to a question on social isolation said that they would value advice, information and support, either greatly (eleven) or a little (five) from a suitably trained and experienced social worker to address this problem. Just two respondents said that they had not experienced social isolation linked with being transgender (Table 5.3). Only one person indicated that they were currently receiving support to address social isolation from a social or care worker, while one other respondent was receiving it from another source. Six people indicated that they had received assistance from a social or care worker or another source to address this problem in the past.

Table 5.3: The value of advice, information and support from an appropriately trained and experienced social worker or care worker to help address social isolation linked with being transgender (Survey two: n = 29).

Valuation of advice, information and support to address social isolation linked with being transgender	Number of respondents	Percentage of respondents
I would value this advice, information and support greatly	11	41
I would value this advice, information and support a little	5	19
I don't know how much I would value this advice, information and support	2	7
I would not value this advice, information and support very much	2	7
I would not value this advice, information and support at all	0	0
Not applicable: I do not need this advice, information and support	5	19
Not applicable: I have not experienced social isolation linked with being transgender	2	7
Total	**27**	**100**

Low respondent numbers (twenty of a possible forty-seven) to a question about health problems or disability linked with being transgender are noticeable when compared with some of the other tables in this series. Nonetheless, counsellors or psychiatrists were rated in the three highest columns of importance by eleven of the twenty respondents as a source of advice and support regarding such health problems or disabilities (Table 5.4). This suggests that the 'health problems or disability linked with being transgender', which were being treated, were of a mental

Table 5.4: The importance of sources of advice or support regarding health problems or disability linked with being transgender (Survey one: n = 47: 20 respondents).

Key: Importance of sources of advice and support regarding health problems or disability linked with transgender condition (1 = highest importance, 11 = least importance).

Source/Importance of advice or support regarding health problems or disability linked with being transgender	1	2	3	4	5	6	7	8	9	10	11
a. Close friends	2	7	0	1	1	1	0	0	1	2	4
b. Family members	5	0	2	2	0	0	3	0	2	0	5
c. Colleagues at work/line manager	1	1	0	1	0	0	0	1	0	2	7
d. Transgender support group	5	1	2	0	2	0	0	2	0	0	3
e. General practitioner	3	1	3	3	0	0	0	0	1	0	3
f. Gender specialist at GIC	2	1	0	1	3	1	0	1	1	0	4
g. Speech therapist	1	0	0	2	0	0	0	0	0	0	5
h. Health visitor or district nurse	0	0	0	0	0	0	1	0	1	0	7
i. Counsellor or psychiatrist	8	1	2	0	2	1	0	0	1	0	3
j. Social worker	1	0	0	0	0	1	0	1	0	1	5
k. Carer/personal assistant/support worker	2	0	0	0	0	0	0	1	0	0	7

A	B	C	D	E	F
16>	11–15	6–10	16>	11–15	6–10

For full explanation of typographic coding, please see table 1.1 on p. 13.

health nature for many respondents, and that a more positive response was experienced by some transgender people with general psychiatrists than others have reported (see, for example, Morton, 2008, pp. 11–18). A further cross-tabulation indicated no significant differences between those respondents in a male role with a male gender identity and those in a female role with a female gender identity regarding support for health problems or disability linked with being transgender (Norman, 2015a, pp. 282–3).

Bearing in mind the concerns noted above that MtF people rated transgender groups less highly than FtM individuals, for assistance with gender identity and transition issues, mainly positive ratings of support from transgender groups were found to be spread fairly evenly between those who were living in a male gender role with a male gender identity, and those who were living in a female gender role with a female gender identity (Norman, 2015a, p. 283).

A three-way cross-tabulation indicated that all four of the respondents in a current male gender role and with a male gender identity rated close friends in the three highest categories for support with health problems or disability linked with being transgender. Conversely, none of the four respondents in a current female gender role and with a female gender identity placed close friends in the three highest categories, while three of the four respondents actually put them in the three lowest categories.

Similarly, a further three-way cross-tabulation indicated that three of the four respondents in a current male gender role and with a male gender identity rated family members in the three highest categories for support with health problems or disability linked with being transgender (with the remaining respondent placing family members in the three lowest categories for such support). Conversely, three of the four respondents in a current female gender role and with a female gender identity rated support from family members in the three lowest categories.

Social and care workers received very low ratings of importance, in general. One interviewee commented on mental health issues from a personal perspective in relation to possible sources of assistance:

Ciaran: 'I have thought about phoning the Samaritans at times but I'm never brave enough and wouldn't know what to say' (Norman, 2015a, p. 278).

While recognising the invaluable service provided by the Samaritans in the UK, it may be that a specialist phone support service might give some transgender people confidence to access phone support. It is possible that phone support services such as the LGBT (Centre for Health and Wellbeing) Helpline Scotland may already meet some of this need.

CHAPTER 6

Support to Family Members

Introduction

> In our culture, the family occupies a central role. For most people, the idea
> of life without some sort of family structure to provide a source of caring,
> comfort and emotional security is unthinkable. We tend to treat the role of
> the family and the value of what it does for the individual as some sort of self-
> evident, obvious truth (Murgatroyd and Woolfe, 1985, pp. 15–16).

While this quote suggests a somewhat idealised view of the family, for
many people it may indeed represent a 'self-evident, obvious truth'
of family structure and support at the heart of their lives. But what
happens when a family has to deal with the highly unusual event of a
transgender person 'coming out', with a gender identity that is incon-
sistent with their apparent biological sex? Biblarz and Savci suggest
that although 'academic research on transgender people and their
family relationships is almost non-existent ... their families have to
adjust to having a relative of another gender, and hence transgender
people undergo a very different kind of coming out' (to that of gay, lesbian and bisexual people) (Biblarz and Savci, 2010, p. 489).

This chapter addresses transgender-related family issues including
the nature and extent of advice and support to family members, particularly to partners and children.

Support and advice in understanding transgender

Difficulties within relationships with partners, including potentially
transphobic attitudes and behaviours, have been partially explored by
the Scottish LGBT Domestic Abuse survey (see Chapter 4 above, and
Roch *et al.*, 2010, p. 15). Additional research has shown, for transgender
people who are parents, that coming out may result in reduced access to
their former partner and to their children. McNeil *et al.* found that, of
188 participants who were parents, 19% reported seeing their child(ren)

less, 18% lost contact with their children and 8% had custody issues. Only 17% found telling their children (about their being transgender) a positive experience (McNeil *et al.,* 2012, p. 90).

Within the Scottish 2015 study just two of the six interviewees indicated that their family had been both understanding and supportive:

> **Andrew:** 'I do have a very supportive family and my parents both understood that I needed to transition' (Norman, 2015a, p. 250).

> **Abigail:** 'At the time, apart from the rather infrequent appointments with the gender specialist, there was no support of any kind available at all … We had to deal with it ourselves. And we did' (Norman, 2015a, p. 245).

However, some families found it hard to adjust to a transgender member coming out, leading to discord and, in some cases, to their potential isolation. One respondent commented:

> **Sarah:** 'I don't communicate with my father. "You're no son of mine!" pretty much sums up his attitude in a dreadfully ironic way … I avoid any contact with the rest of my family … with the exception of my mother, I don't think they want to even acknowledge me as a family member, let alone include me' (Norman, 2015a, p. 250).

One interviewee explained:

> **Luke:** 'My mum in particular found my transition very hard and she would have liked to talk to someone about this – particularly the rejection from her brother and his wife. They now ignore me at family gatherings etc. and she finds this very hard. Mum also felt that family help would have been good so my brother, sister and dad could have talked about what they were feeling. Although it was only me transitioning, everyone had their own thoughts and feelings on the matter' (Norman, 2015a, p. 404).

One interviewee found his siblings to be supportive, though his father was less so :

Ciaran: 'My ... sisters actually coped the best looking back on it now; they just accepted my new name and whenever anyone would slip up with my name they would be the first to correct them which always put a smile on my face' (Norman, 2015a, p. 408).

'When I gave him the last birthday card signed in my new name, he told me to "pack it in, it's not funny anymore"' (Norman, 2015a, p. 409).

Another interviewee described the rejection of her 'in laws':

Kay: (My wife's) 'family have been completely unaccepting, and no amount of support workers would ever help that' (Norman, 2015a, p. 394).

It might be conjectured that a family's concerns about how society in general views transgender people may be influenced by prejudice and transphobia, leading to embarrassment or shame. Fear of the family becoming a source of gossip or of rejection by extended family members, neighbours, friends, colleagues and/or acquaintances might be part of the amalgam of these concerns. There may be other feelings too, of guilt or of loss (of a son or daughter, of a partner or of a parent).

Two of the interviewees within the Scottish 2015 study put down their thoughts on 'loss' – to themselves, and to family members too:

Sarah: 'I "lost" my family long before transition (but) if anything, it's brought my mother and I closer' (Norman, 2015a, p. 261).

Ciaran: 'I know my mum struggled with the "loss" of a daughter/potential grandchildren and my 13 year old sister was also quite upset, but once they came to realise I was the same person inside and much happier they found it easier to move forward from those feelings' (Norman, 2015a, p. 261).

One interviewee noted religious reasons for her family's rejection:

Josie: 'My immediate family, mainly my mother and for that matter my mother in law, are of a very strong religious belief and to an extent what I have done was against their belief system and therefore (they) cannot accept it on that basis' (Norman, 2015a, p. 261).

In addition, accurate, factual information about transgender may not be readily available to family members, or there may be no one outwith the family with whom the subject can be discussed. (Benvenuto, in her account of her experiences relating to her partner's transition, displays a fairly comprehensive overview of transsexuality, including consideration of gender, gender identity, transgender and aetiology though this may be exceptional (Benvenuto, 2012, pp. 157–66).) For the child of a transgender parent, there may be a fear of being rejected or being made fun of by one's peer group, or by one's teachers. However, Benvenuto suggests the 'literature about the transsexual experience plays down or altogether omits the loss experienced by a child whose parent changes gender' (Benvenuto, 2012, p. 11).

Three interviewees shed light on how both close and extended members of a family may struggle with transition:

> **Ciaran:** 'None of my family received support in the professional sense but they supported each other at times. I think my mum and my aunt … would have benefited the most from additional support as they did struggle a bit to accept my decision. My aunt spent many hours trying to persuade me it was "just a phase and I would regret it" but once she realised how serious I was she vowed to support me no matter what. If they had had support they could have discussed how to deal with nosy people quizzing them, to voice their disapproving comments and maybe help them understand how I was feeling mentally as I wasn't very good at vocalising my thoughts/feelings' (Norman, 2015a, pp. 251–2).

> **Lucy:** 'My mother had real problems with my gender change … back then information was not readily available. She went to her GP to find out more. However he was not willing to discuss the matter, so she went to the library. However I gather they were most unhelpful, considering transsexualism as something weird and pornographic' (Norman, 2015a, p. 252).

Suzie: 'At the time of my transition, there was only the (GIC) that I was aware of ... I think that they had a support group for both parties. Everyone needs support, not just people transitioning. Though my family were supportive at the time, I could not explain how I felt and make them understand' (Norman, 2015a, p. 252).

Working with families

Murgatroyd and Woolfe suggest that working with a family is very different from working with an individual because 'families have their own dynamics, their own structures and strategies and their own "games" by which the contributions of the individuals within the family are mediated' and in discussing 'the role of a helper in a family crisis' they suggest that 'an event ... may be perceived as a crisis by one family but as a hiccup or a non-problem by another family'. They suggest that most families learn from earlier experiences and develop 'anticipatory coping skills' but for the family faced with the news that one of their members is transgender (or has changed or is changing gender role imminently) there may be little time to adjust and to use existing coping resources (Murgatroyd and Woolfe, 1985, pp. 5, 119, 126).

Brown and Rounsley explain the background to such a potential family crisis when they describe how:

> most transsexuals reach the point where their gender dysphoria dominates their lives to such an overwhelming extent that daily functioning becomes difficult if not impossible ... debilitating depression often sets in ... they cannot ignore or deny their gender dysphoria any longer: something has to change.

They describe how 'the news is especially hard for family members and close friends to accept – they are usually profoundly confused and distressed ... the old rules no longer apply' (Brown and Rounsley, 2003, pp. 5, 96).

The pressure on other family members, particularly partners, at such a time of crisis for the transgender person is likely to be very great indeed. Lev suggests that:

> a few clinicians have noted that families of transgender people move through a (four) stage process that is as predictable as the

one Kubler-Ross outlined in her work with patients addressing issues of death and dying.

The four stages are described by Lev as: 'discovery and disclosure' (usually involving a sense of shock or confusion); 'turmoil' (a time of intense stress and conflict); 'negotiation' (including adjustment, compromise and recognition of new boundaries for gender expression); and 'finding balance' (being ready to integrate the transgender person back into the normative life of the family) (Lev, 2006, pp. 267, 269). By helping a family to recognise these four stages a support worker might be able to identify where the family has reached in coming to terms with the presence of a transgender member, and to clarify how best to assist them, as a group and as individuals, to progress their acceptance of new developments.

Family support of a transgender person may vary significantly according to the individual family member's relationship to the transgender person: for example, the support needs of the partner or children of a transgender adult are likely to be rather different from those of the parents or siblings of a transgender child. Similarly, the needs of members of the more extended family such as grandparents, aunts and uncles, cousins, nephews and nieces may vary (additionally perhaps according to their gender or age, and other factors including religion).

Partners and children

The specific needs of partners or children of a transgender person should be considered separately from that of other family members, for they are likely to be the most vulnerable close relations, although their needs, coping mechanisms and the long-term effects of transition on their relationships have been inadequately researched to date.

Like Lev (2006), Cohen *et al.* note that 'the process of adjustment for spouses of GLBT (*sic*) people involves three general stages: shock, anger and confusion'. These stages presuppose a lack of openness from the transgender partner about their gender identity earlier in the relationship: in this case, the fundamental nature of the original relationship may become subject to doubt and redefinition. The physical and relational natures of transition also have to be negotiated, during which 'the expectations and conceptions that intimate partners hold concerning the identity of their transsexual partners are deeply challenged as they see their physical and other transformations' (Cohen *et al.*, 2006, pp. 164–5). Partners may value separate and individualised support and counselling to help them through these twin readjustments. As two of the interviewees within the Scottish 2015 study explained:

> **Andrew:** 'My partner ... did not receive any support. She had many questions, some of which I could not answer. It was also difficult to be so wrapped up in my own transition and having to support my partner at the same time (who had the same sort of problem, having to come to terms with me transitioning and supporting me at the same time). I am sure she would have very much appreciated somebody to talk to who was not involved in my transition. There is very little support even online for partners and families (Norman, 2015a, p. 398).

> **Kay:** 'I was married when I came out, and my wife listened to what I had to say, but again would have greatly appreciated an external source of knowledgeable discussion about the basic facts of transgender. It was very emotional at first, and she (spent time) by herself ... to think. On her return she was very keen to engage in what was happening with me and she made a remarkable effort to research and (to) understand what transgender is ... I think support workers for spouses are often overlooked. We have both used (a support website) enormously ... they have a forum section for spouses and partners and in the early days I know my wife found it helpful to chat with other spouses of trans-people' (Norman, 2015a, p. 395).

Cohen *et al.* quote Davis (2002), who notes that 'those who lived with their partners during the pre-transition period found the transition process confusing. Thus they frequently continued to see their partner in their gender of birth, or in some unique combination of masculine or feminine characteristics ... intimate partners must also re-examine their own sexuality in light of the revelation of their partner's transsexuality ... ultimately while some relationships dissolve, many non-transsexual partners remain involved as co-parents, non-intimate partners, or intimate partners' (Cohen *et al.*, 2006, p. 165).

Barrett notes the distinction between the majority of heterosexual (in the main biologically male) transsexuals and 'a rather smaller proportion of' homosexual transsexuals, whose pre-transition sexual paths differ considerably (and whose post-transition prognoses are likely to differ somewhat too: see the section on Follow-up studies and reviews in Chapter 5). He compares these experiences with biologically female transsexuals for whom 'most have either no history of sexual relations with males, or report a single episode of such sexual interaction' (Barrett, 2007, pp. 19, 22–7).

The NHS/Glasgow University Scottish Transgender Survey found that 'none of the transmen had been married or had children, but two thirds of the transwomen had been married and half had children' (Wilson *et al.*, 2005, p. 2). The widespread nature of such marriages may explain the later average age of transition of MtF transgender people compared to those who are FtM. It seems that many MtF people in particular are likely to try to 'make it work' as a man, before a 'middle age crisis' leads to an acceptance of the fundamental nature of their gender dysphoria (Brown and Rounsley, 2003, pp. 96–7).

From a child's perspective, Brown and Rounsley suggest that 'the impact (of disclosure of transgender status in a parent) is largely dependent on their parents and possibly the immediate family. If adults in their environment are bitter or hostile about the situation, angry at the transsexual, and secretive, as if shielding others from some despicable or criminal act, children are without a doubt negatively affected. They can become depressed, anxious and conflicted. They note that:

> as a rule, prepubescent kids can handle the transition well as long as the other parent and family members don't undermine the transsexual parent (but that) if kids are adolescents … it can be more difficult to deal with.

Brown and Rounsley suggest that a fear of losing friends, or being the focus of gossip, or feelings of embarrassment or shame might also extend to a sense of anger and depression in a transgender person's child/ren. They suggest that particular care needs to be provided by supportive professionals, of whom social workers may well be most experienced in family work, to ensure that the nature of a child's relationship with their transsexual parent is a potential topic for advice, discussion and support if needed (Brown and Rounsley, 2003, pp. 190–2).

Much of the above discussion has centred round the scenario of an adult transsexual person 'coming out' to their family. However, increasingly, transgender children and young people make their condition known while still living at home, though there may be limited local support (exacerbated by the lack of local GIC support for them – transgender children in Scotland, for example, need a GP referral to the Tavistock centre in London). Brill and Pepper note the developmental stages of the transgender child, including the trauma of puberty and describe a process of family acceptance, 'from crisis to empowerment' (Brill and Pepper, 2008, pp. 39–59, 64–71), which bears some similarity to the stages outlined by Lev (2006) and by Cohen *et al.* (2006) above, and which might be used to underpin social support to a transgender child and their family.

Similarly, within a detailed 'summary of recommendations for the clinical treatment of transgender and gender variant youth' Mallon includes a section on 'supporting transgender emergence in adolescence', which might also form a useful framework for social work support (Mallon, 2009, pp. 179–80). This, together with a comprehensive chapter that considers social work practice with transgender and gender variant children and youth (Mallon and DeCrescenzo, 2009, pp. 65–86), provides a thoughtful account of the likely issues facing a transgender child, their family and their social or care worker, containing a section of recommendations or implications for practice, which ends with the sobering thought that:

> practitioners must accept the reality that not everyone can provide validation for a transgender child or teen. Some will simply not be able to understand the turmoil and pain transgender children and youth experience. In these instances, practitioners must be prepared to advocate vigorously on behalf of these youths (Mallon and DeCrescenzo, 2009, pp. 79–82).

Follow-up studies suggest that 'compared with the adult group ... adolescents function better psychologically (Kuiper, 1991). In addition, they appear to have far fewer social problems and they receive much more support from their families and friends' (Cohen-Kettenis and van Goozen, 1997, p. 270). However, Jeffreys quotes from Pepper who makes the pertinent comment that, 'as children transition, so too must their families' (Pepper, 2012, p. xviii, in Jeffreys, 2014, p. 98).

Advice and support about transition

One of the most important findings within the Scottish 2015 study was just how few families received support about their relative's gender role transition: thirty (69%) families had received no advice or support at all (Table 6.1, Norman, 2015a, p. 252).

Table 6.1: The provision of advice or support to family members about a gender role transition (Survey one: n = 47).

Advice or support received by family member(s) about a gender role transition	Number of respondents	Percentage of respondents
None of my family received advice or support	30	69
My parent(s) received advice or support	3	7
My sibling(s) received advice or support	1	2
My partner received advice or support	2	5
My child(ren) received advice or support	3	7
My wider family received advice or support	0	0
Not applicable: I am not making/have not made/do not intend to make a gender role transition	2	5
Other*	2	5
Total	**43**	**100**

***Other:** '(It) would have been good if my mother hadn't had to deal with understanding all this herself when I was growing up.' 'My mum had psychologist support from children and young people's gender clinic and from Mermaids group, my dad and brothers were offered but didn't accept support from the psychologist and gender clinic for children and young people.'

Cross-tabulating age with support to family members showed that the response 'none of my family received advice or support' was given by fewer people in the combined age groups 16–25 and 26–35, than by those aged 36–45 and 46–55. Three young people aged 16–25 indicated that their parents had received advice or support – the only age group to report support to their parents. Three people across the combined categories 36–45 and 46–55 indicated that their children had received advice or support, and one person aged over 66 said that their sibling had received support. The partners of two people (each of whom was aged over forty-five years) had also received advice and support on this matter (Norman, 2015a, p. 253).

Cross-tabulating current gender role with support to family members about transition indicated broadly similar ratios of family members who had received no support for those respondents in current gender roles of male (ten of fifteen), female (fourteen of twenty-one), transgender (three of seven) and 'other' (two of three) (Norman, 2105, p. 253). One anonymous survey respondent commented on the scarcity of such support:

> 'My wife ... would have greatly appreciated an external source of knowledgeable discussion about the basic facts of transgender ... I think support workers for spouses are often overlooked' (Norman, 2105, p. 253).

Two interviewees explained the difficulties for their partners and the possible role a social worker might have taken:

> **Andrew**: 'A social worker could have simply been available for a chat when things got difficult. We are both independent and strong people but knowing that there is somebody who can listen to your thoughts, who is not your partner, can be very helpful' (Norman, 2015a, p. 253).

> **Josie**: 'The involvement of my wife at an earlier stage of the ... process would have been beneficial ... (she) was only brought into the formal process on the last interview before my operation' (Norman, 2015a, p. 254).

Sources of support to family members in coming to terms with transition

Just fourteen respondents (of a possible forty-seven) rated the importance of a range of sources of advice or support to family members in coming to terms with transition, which perhaps reflects the paucity of such support during transition. Despite these low overall response rates, transgender support groups were still placed in the three highest categories as a source of advice and support regarding helping family members to come to terms with a gender transition by over a half of respondents (eight of the fourteen). Other family members, close friends, gender specialists, GPs and counsellors or psychiatrists received mixed ratings from both high to low importance (Lev even suggests that 'the clinical philosophy of most gender specialists has been to view family members as extraneous to the process of evaluation and treatment'; Lev, 2006,

p. 263). Most respondents rated colleagues at work and line managers as of low importance as a source of support at this time. Five respondents considered the support from social workers and care workers quite highly, although over twice as many (twelve) placed social work support in the three lowest categories (Table 6.2; Norman, 2015a, p. 254).

The absence of a consistently reliable and available source of advice and support to the immediate families of transgender people, to their partners or parents, or to their children or siblings, is of particular concern at a time when family support structures are likely to be themselves most threatened. As the NHS/Glasgow University Survey found:

> experiences surrounding gender transition ranged from remarkable levels of support to total rejection and threats of violence ... family support was often lacking at times of most need ... problems with families were almost universal among ... respondents (Wilson *et al.*, 2005, p. 27).

Some respondents clearly empathised with the needs of families at this time:

> **Lucy**: 'I believe family members, parents and siblings need someone whom they can talk to, (to) find out more and discuss their fears and worries with. It must be quite a shock to suddenly find (that) a person whom you may have given birth to is not quite the person you thought they were. I think in this situation an experienced social/care worker would be perceived as a neutral person, someone who can be trusted with no particular axe to grind' (Norman, 2015a, p. 256).

Brown and Rounsley note that:

> coming out to family members is usually much more difficult for transsexuals than coming out at work ... the thought of rejection by family members ... can be devastating ... there are few losses greater than that of the family bond (Brown and Rounsley, 2003, p. 167).

Jeffreys quotes Erhardt's (2007) findings that 'initial reactions range from bewilderment and disbelief to shock and then embarrassment at the thought of others finding out' (Jeffreys, 2014, p. 85), while also recognising Erhardt's perspective that:

Table 6.2: The importance of sources of advice or support in helping family members come to terms with transition
(Survey one: n = 47: 14 respondents).

Key: Importance of sources of advice and support to family regarding gender role transition (1 = highest importance, 11 = least importance).

Source/Importance of advice or support in helping family members come to terms with transition	1	2	3	4	5	6	7	8	9	10	11
a. Close friends	4	2	2	0	0	1	0	0	0	0	5
b. Family members	2	2	1	0	2	0	0	0	0	0	6
c. Colleagues at work/line manager	1	0	2	0	0	0	1	0	0	0	7
d. Transgender support group	5	1	2	0	0	0	1	0	0	0	2
e. General practitioner	4	1	0	0	1	1	0	0	0	0	4
f. Gender specialist at GIC	2	2	0	0	0	1	0	1	0	0	4
g. Speech therapist	2	0	0	0	0	1	0	1	0	0	5
h. Health visitor or district nurse	1	0	0	0	0	1	0	0	1	0	6
i. Counsellor or psychiatrist	4	1	0	1	0	1	0	0	0	1	3
j. Social worker	2	0	0	0	0	1	0	0	0	1	5
k. Carer/personal assistant/support worker	2	1	0	0	0	1	0	0	0	0	6

For full explanation of typographic coding, please see table 1.1 on p. 13.

A	B	C	D	E	F
16>	11–15	6–10	16>	11–15	6–10

it is extremely important … to remember that being a person of transgender experience is involuntary. I have heard women who leave (their partner) insist on believing that their partner was frivolously choosing a transgender lifestyle (Erhardt, 2007, p. 6, from Jeffreys, 2014, p. 83).

Family acceptance of a transgender member predicts greater self-esteem, social support and general status, so working through family difficulties at this time will almost certainly ensure better outcomes for both the transgender person and their family (Ryan *et al.*, 2010, p. 205). Another interviewee commented on the potential value of family support groups:

> **Suzie**: 'Someone who had an outside knowledge could explain transition from a non-judgemental view-point. Your family still expect to see the same person, regardless of the physical changes, emotional changes etc. We don't all follow the same path. Family support groups, if the families use them, can put the points across better than we can, about acceptance and respect. Families may feel more at ease, talking to other people (in a group) or a one to one talk' (Norman, 2015a, p. 256).

As Hines notes, 'the partnering and parenting relationships of transgender people are ignored not just within sociologies of the family, but also within gender research' (Hines, 2007, p. 127); it is clear from the above discussion that wider availability of advice and support from professional, knowledgeable sources is a much-needed addition to existing services. This point of view is supported by the feedback of twelve of twenty-seven respondents within the current research, who felt that their partner or other family member would value such support greatly (ten) or a little (two), although approximately a quarter (seven of twenty-seven) said that their partners or other family members did not need this support (Table 6.3; Norman, 2015a, p. 256).

A cross-tabulation with age indicated a slight tendency to a greater need for information and support in families of younger transgender people: four of the seven people in the age group 16–25 thought that one or more members of their family would value this assistance greatly, with six of the eighteen respondents aged twenty-six or over also saying this (Norman, 2015a, p. 257).

Table 6.3: The value of advice, information and support from an appropriately trained and experienced social worker or care worker to help partners or other family better understand about being transgender and/or the consequences of transitioning (Survey two: n = 29).

Valuation of advice, information and support to partners/family to help them understand about transgender/making a transition	Number of respondents	Percentage of respondents
One or more would value this advice, information and support greatly	10	37
One or more would value this advice, information and support a little	2	7
I don't know how much they would value advice, information and support	5	19
None would value this advice, information and support very much	2	7
None would value this advice, information and support at all	1	4
Not applicable: none needs this advice, information and support	7	26
Total	**27**	**100**

Surprisingly, given the apparent disparity between family support to FtM and MtF people, in regard to gender identity and transition issues noted earlier, the ten people who thought that their family members would value transgender information/advice greatly were spread fairly equally between those who were biologically male and female and living in female and male gender roles respectively (Norman, 2015a, p. 257).

The need for support for the partners of those who transition from FtM within a lesbian relationship was also identified within the Scottish 2015 study, although one interviewee described the generally positive experiences of coming out to both his partner, and his partner's family:

> **Ciaran:** 'I met my fiancée when we were (in our teens) and we're now (in our twenties). She just accepted it and carried on loving me for me but I think additional support or information booklets instead of the confusing information online would have made things easier for her too ... since our engagement I am always invited to family functions, we pop in once a week to the in-laws for a cuppy or stay for tea and they come over to our

flat for cakes and a catch up. However I think they would have benefited (from) some reading material, to better understand my position' (Norman, 2015a, pp. 257–8).

Some interviewees' families were clearly supportive, even without support themselves:

> **Andrew**: 'My family did not receive any support. I do have a very supportive family and my parents both understood that I needed to transition. They, and my sister, said that I had always been a bit awkward and that it all made sense now. My grandmother and great aunt (both in their eighties!) also accepted quickly that I needed to transition' (Norman, 2015a, p. 258).

Social care support

One interviewee explained the problem of trying to deal with family concerns on their own, and the potential value of impartial support:

> **Kay**: 'The biggest battle with my family was in explaining what transgender is and means: the difference between cross-dressing, transvestites, androgyne and transsexual. Attempting to convince them that I am not a pervert in any way, that dressing as female is not a sexual thing at all for me, that it is identity and internal make up, not kink. This was a steep battle, particularly as my mum is a very strong Christian.
>
> 'A support worker could have taken some of this basic explaining work off me, particularly because I was the subject issue … my mum in particular was desperate to talk with a medical authority, and would not, and still does not, really believe I am serious. In many ways my explanation and interpretation of the transsexual landscape was treated with caution because I was trying to describe it in relation to myself and so was biased, whereas had an impartial, knowledgeable, external party explained it they would have been trusted instantly' (Norman, 2015a, p. 258).

Twenty-six of twenty-nine respondents (96%) indicated that their family members were not receiving advice and support to come to terms with a transition from a social or care worker at present, while just three people indicated that members of their family had received this assistance in the past from a social or care worker. One respondent explained that 'members of my family have received some advice from support groups and my gender specialist, and value this advice very much' (Norman, 2015a, pp. 258–9). One interviewee commented that:

> **Ciaran:** 'I think any form of family support/therapy from an appropriately trained person would be extremely valuable, especially when younger family members are involved (Norman, 2015a, p. 261).

In response to a further survey question, fourteen of twenty-seven respondents said that they would value advice and information greatly (ten) or a little (four) to help family members better understand and/or address differences concerning being transgender/transitioning. A third of participants (nine) said that they did not need such advice and support, while just one of the twenty-seven respondents said that they had not experienced such family differences (Table 6.4; Norman, 2015a, p. 259).

Table 6.4: The value of advice, information and support from an appropriately trained and experienced social worker or care worker to help partners, children and/or other family members better understand and/or address differences, disagreements or conflicts concerning being transgender and/or the consequences of transitioning (Survey two: n = 29).

Valuation of advice, information and support to help family members understand/address differences about the respondent being transgender	Number of respondents	Percentage of respondents
I would value this advice, information and support greatly	10	37
I would value this advice, information and support a little	4	15
I don't know how much I would value this advice, information and support	2	7
I would not value this advice, information and support very much	1	4
I would not value this advice, information and support at all	0	0
Not applicable: I do not need this advice, information and support	9	33
Not applicable: I have not experienced such family differences, disagreements or conflicts linked with being transgender, or transitioning	1	4
Total	**27**	**100**

A cross-tabulation with age indicated that, of the ten people who would value this assistance greatly, three were in the age group 16–25 while the remaining seven were spread across the combined age groups 26–35, 36–45, and 46–55 (Norman, 2015a, p. 260).

One interviewee described how other members of her family might respond to an offer of support:

> **Amy**: 'You asked me if a specialist trained social worker would (have) helped some of my relatives come to accept and understand my transition from M-F? The answer is an emphatic no! I tried to explain to my brother five years ago and he just swore at me. He and his family do not acknowledge my existence; his son turns his head away from me … he wanted my mother to tell me to leave … home because I would be an embarrassment to him and his family by association … however my mother and father said "no" to him and have supported me' (Norman, 2015a, p. 261).

One survey respondent indicated that assistance with such disagreements or conflicts had been received in the past, and had been valued greatly, while another stated that 'members of my family value advice given from my GP and from my gender specialist'. However, twenty-six (96%) of participants indicated that such support was not being received at present from a social or care worker, and twenty-four people (89%) noted that such assistance had not been received in the past (Norman, 2015a, p. 260). One interviewee explained the damage that can be done through non-acceptance:

> **Ciaran**: 'Maybe if there had been someone my dad could have spoken (with) he wouldn't have publicly disowned me and proceeded to tell anyone and everyone he meets that know me only (by my male name) that I was in fact a "girl" and my real name was (original female name), which not only put the person in an awkward position but led to more people whispering/pointing … and posting horrible things online' (Norman, 2015a, p. 262).

CHAPTER 7

Transgender and Society

Introduction

This chapter consists of an exploration and discussion of the findings of the Scottish 2015 study into support for transgender people in relation to changing documentation, social rejection, post GIC support, and support related to relationships with friends, neighbours and colleagues. It includes consideration of how transgender people might be supported in developing a more confident community presence, and finding a place within a society which, though apparently increasingly curious and knowledgeable of transgender matters, may nonetheless be uncertain how to accommodate this unusual and infrequently encountered minority group.

Changing documentation

> **Abigail:** 'There is a huge host of practical things – changing NHS card, NI number, passport, bank accounts … the list is endless, and I still haven't got to the bottom of it all (insurance policies are a particular nightmare) where social work guidance would be invaluable. I feel I blundered through, and continue to blunder through, a hugely complex process with all kinds of practical implications I am almost completely ignorant of' (Norman, 2015a, p. 266).

Whittle suggests that 'for transsexual and transgender people who commence living permanently in their preferred gender role the changing of one's documentation is a crucial part of the transition process' (Whittle, 2008, p. 2). Changing documentation is also an essential part of the real-life test unless the transgender person is to face potential daily discord between gender-related documentation and gender attribution. Several interviewees and survey respondents explained that the formal process of changing name and gender in documentation with a wide range of organisations had proved a time-consuming and, at times, frustratingly complex process, which probably corresponded with a time of intense personal stress immediately prior to, during or just after a very public gender transition.

When asked to rate a list of sources of advice or support in order of their importance with 'helping you to change your documentation', transgender support groups were rated as of the highest importance by more than half of participants (eighteen of thirty-three), with just four people rating them of low importance. Gender specialists at a gender identity clinic received mixed ratings from both high to low importance. Six respondents viewed GPs as the most important source of advice and support (this may have been linked with the provision of a letter by the GP confirming gender role reassignment which the respondent was then able to copy and send to organisations etc.). Overall, equal numbers (twelve) placed GPs in the three highest categories of importance as in the three lowest categories. Social and care workers received very low ratings of importance in general (Table 7.1; Norman, 2015a, p. 263):

Some 52% (fourteen) of twenty-seven participants said that they would value assistance from an appropriately trained and experienced social worker or care worker to help them 'to change documentation prior to, during or following a gender transition', either greatly or a little, while ten (37%) participants said that they did not need such assistance (Table 7.2; Norman, 2015a, p. 264).

One respondent suggested that:

> **Kay:** 'A pre-prepared mail pack or pdf could be sent to transitioning individuals, explaining the process, who to get in touch with etc' (Norman, 2015a, p. 267).

A cross-tabulation of this question indicated that those who would value this assistance greatly were fairly evenly spread across most age ranges. Seven of twelve biological males and six of ten biological females said that they would value this information either greatly or a little. Six people said that they had received assistance with documentation in the past from a social or care worker, while three people indicated that this had been received from another source.

Table 7.1: The importance of sources of advice or support in helping to change documentation to assist with transition
(Survey one: n = 47: 33 respondents).

Key: Importance of sources of advice and support regarding legal and personal documentation (1 = highest importance, 11 = least importance).

Source/Importance of advice or support in helping to change documentation to assist with transition	1	2	3	4	5	6	7	8	9	10	11
a. Close friends	4	1	2	0	1	2	2	0	0	3	13
b. Family members	3	1	0	2	4	2	1	0	0	3	14
c. Colleagues at work/line manager	3	2	4	1	2	1	0	1	1	2	12
d. Transgender support group	18	3	1	1	2	0	0	1	1	2	4
e. General practitioner	6	4	2	1	0	1	1	2	0	1	11
f. Gender specialist at GIC	9	3	4	3	1	1	0	0	0	1	11
g. Speech therapist	3	0	0	0	2	3	0	1	1	2	14
h. Health visitor or district nurse	1	0	0	0	1	1	1	1	1	2	18
i. Counsellor or psychiatrist	4	1	4	1	1	0	1	2	0	2	12
j. Social worker	2	0	1	0	1	1	2	0	2	3	14
k. Carer/personal assistant/support worker	2	0	1	0	1	1	0	0	0	5	16

For full explanation of typographic coding, please see table 1.1 on p. 13.

A	B	C	D	E	F
16>	11–15	6–10	16>	11–15	6–10

Table 7.2: The value of advice, information and support from an appropriately trained and experienced social worker or care worker to change documentation prior to, during or following a gender transition (Survey two: n = 29).

Valuation of advice, information and support to help change documentation prior to, during or following a gender transition	Number of respondents	Percentage of respondents
I would value this advice, information and support greatly	12	45
I would value this advice, information and support a little	2	7
I don't know how much I would value this advice, information and support	2	7
I would not value this advice, information and support very much	1	4
I would not value this advice, information and support at all	0	0
Not applicable: I do not need this advice, information and support	10	37
Total	**27**	**100**

For some interviewees the process of changing documentation had proved difficult and complex:

> **Luke:** 'Because I had no help I ended up filling out the paper work three or four times over, which made what should (have) been a quick and simple process very hard. For some things like the bank it was straightforward, (whilst changing my) passport … wasn't. I know of a lot of trans-people who have not a clue how to get them. I only figured it out by googling it, which, as always, brought up completely useless information as well as helpful – I just had to figure out which was which' (Norman, 2015a, p. 265).

> **Andrew:** 'When I considered changing my documentation I first asked my GP but he had no help to offer. I then researched the topic online and found several contradictory sources. Eventually I changed my name through an online service and then changed my driving licence so that I could use that as proof of ID when changing all my other documentation. I did not tick a box for either female or male as I was going to ask when handing

in the form which box I legally need to tick. On handing over the form at the DVLA the woman quickly glanced at me and ticked "male". I left it at that' (Norman, 2015a, p. 266).

Two interviewees noted difficulties with the health board amending its records to reflect their altered gender status:

Lucy: 'My main gripe is with my local health board who are obstructive and downright rude. In inter-board communications I am referred to as a "male patient" even now. This makes me angry. I complain, the board apologises and then just simply carries on' (Norman, 2015a, p. 266).

Luke: 'I have also had numerous run-ins with certain departments of the NHS ... with some refusing to call me Luke or being called Miss Luke' (Norman, 2015a, p. 266).

Gender recognition certificate

Although twenty-seven of forty-seven respondents to a survey question within the Scottish 2015 study had changed their gender role to match their gender identity, only thirteen of these had applied for and received a GRC; two more had an application in progress. Nine of the remaining twenty participants were in the process of transition (Norman, 2015a, p. 267).

Cross-tabulating age with other data for those who had received a GRC indicated a fairly even distribution across all age groups, with a similarly even spread across all age groups for those participants who had not applied for the certificate. However, a three-way cross-tabulation between current gender role, gender identity and applications for a GRC indicated that, of the ten people living in a male role who described their gender identity as male, six had applied for and received a GRC. Conversely, only three of the sixteen people living in a female role who described their gender identity as female had made an application, two of whom had been successful, and one of whom had an application pending (Norman, 2015a, p. 267).

Fifteen of twenty-seven participants said that they would greatly value assistance from an appropriately trained and experienced social worker or care worker when applying for a GRC' (Table 7.3; Norman,

Table 7.3: The value of advice, information and support from an appropriately trained and experienced social worker or care worker to apply for a Gender Recognition Certificate (Survey two: n = 29).

Valuation of advice, information and support to help apply for a Gender Recognition Certificate	Number of respondents	Percentage of respondents
I would value this advice, information and support greatly	15	55
I would value this advice, information and support a little	1	4
I don't know how much I would value this advice, information and support	3	11
I would not value this advice, information and support very much	0	0
I would not value this advice, information and support at all	0	0
Not applicable: I do not need this advice, information and support	8	30
Total	**27**	**100**

2015a, p. 268). A cross-tabulation with age indicated that those who said that they would value this assistance greatly were spread fairly evenly across the age ranges 16–25 through to 46–55. Seven of twelve biological males and seven of ten biological females commented that they would value this information either greatly or a little.

Just two people indicated that they were currently receiving support from a social or care worker with an application for a GRC, while two people said that they had received this assistance in the past.

Social rejection

Lucy: '(My home town) in 19xx was not a welcoming place for transsexuals. I was spat at, beaten up, refused service in shops ... because of my gender change, humiliated in public, had excrement pushed through my letterbox. I soon learned not to ask the police for help; they on one occasion stood by and watched me get beaten. When injured in such cases I soon learnt to avoid the local A&E who were quite judgemental and made it quite plain that if I lived as I did what else could I expect' (Norman, 2015a, p. 298).

As discussed in Chapter 4, the STA survey of 2007 reported that transgender people are regularly concerned about harassment through abusive and transphobic behaviours (Morton, 2008, p. 11). In response to a question within the Scottish 2015 study, twelve of twenty-seven respondents indicated that they would greatly value the advice of a social worker to address the consequences of societal rejection and/or abuse linked with being transgender, with a further four saying that they would value such advice a little. Just two of these twenty-seven respondents said that they had not experienced social rejection/abuse linked with being transgender (Table 7.4; Norman, 2015a, p. 297).

Table 7.4: The value of advice, information and support from an appropriately trained and experienced social worker or care worker to address the consequences of social rejection and/or abuse linked with being transgender (Survey two: n = 29).

Valuation of advice, information and support to help address rejection/abuse linked with being transgender	Number of respondents	Percentage of respondents
I would value this advice, information and support greatly	12	45
I would value this advice, information and support a little	4	15
I don't know how much I would value this advice, information and support	3	11
I would not value this advice, information and support very much	0	0
I would not value this advice, information and support at all	0	0
Not applicable: I do not need this advice, information and support	6	22
Not applicable: I have not experienced social rejection/abuse linked with being transgender	2	7
Total	**27**	**100**

A cross-tabulation of this question with age indicated that the numbers of those who would value this assistance greatly tended to rise gradually with age, up to the age group 46–55, but when those who would value this assistance a little were included this evened out these age differences almost completely.

A further three-way cross-tabulation indicated that three of ten respondents currently living in a male gender role, seven of twelve respondents in a female gender role (each of whom described themselves as having a matching gender identity), one in a transgender role and one in an 'other' role said that they would value such advice greatly (Norman, 2015a, p. 298).

Just one person said that they were currently receiving support with social rejection from a social or care worker, while three people indicated that they had received this assistance in the past. One anonymous survey respondent commented:

> 'I would have valued this greatly, if it had been available to me as a teenager' (Norman, 2015a, p. 298).

Mitchell and Howarth in their trans-research review reported that 'health and social care issues included isolation' (Mitchell and Howarth, 2009, p. 62), and, as noted in Chapter 5, social isolation may be a significant contributor to mental ill health for those who are transgender. Yet almost none of the twenty-seven respondents to the second survey of the Scottish 2015 study were receiving any support for issues of social rejection.

The effects of social isolation may be as pervasive as the effects of transphobia, and the most significant effect of intermittent transphobic incidents may be the increasing reclusion of the transgender person. Several handbooks on social care to transgender people explore the issue of social isolation in some detail, particularly in relation to youth and adolescents. Davis suggests that:

> social isolation may be considered one of the most significant and dangerous aspects of a trans identity ... identification with one's cultural group is a significant component in the development of an individual's self-concept ... (and yet) ... positive trans role models are rare ... when trans people do appear in the media it is often in a pejorative sense ... as sex-workers, freaks, self-mutilators (Davis, 2009, p. 16).

McNeil *et al.* found that just over a half of 'respondents felt that the way trans people were represented in the media had a negative effect on their emotional wellbeing' (McNeil *et al.,* 2012, p. 90).

In a review of 'cross dressing, sex-changing and the press' King suggests press interest is high in transvestite and transgender matters because they question the natural 'fit' of sex, gender and gender presentation, so that 'the general public may be misled or misinformed but it may also be educated and enlightened'. Such exposure, however, 'is a double-edged sword … (for) … 'individual transvestites and transsexuals may be damaged by the exposure they receive' (King, 1996, pp. 133–50).

One interviewee commented on the role of the media in the public perception of transgender people:

> **Lucy:** 'The media, well they take one step forward and then two back. They could be part of the solution but at the same time they are part of the problem. Some papers in particular treat transsexuals as a commodity – I've been door stepped by the national press. Did they want to hear about my politics? – no. My sex life? – yes. A long way to go …' (Norman, 2015a, p. 299).

Post gender identity clinic support

The need for support during the period after transition, when GIC support is no longer available, was a subject raised in the Scottish 2015 pilot study focus group. Billings and Urban pre-empt the likelihood of post-transition difficulties when they note Hastings' quote (Hastings, 1974, p. 337) that 'rarely does such a patient initiate a realistic discussion about the obvious problems that follow surgery: legal, social, economic and emotional' (Billings and Urban, 1996, p. 107). It is likely, however, that in the intervening forty years, particularly with the increasing role of information sharing and discussion forums online, such apparent naivety has been replaced in the minds of many transgender people with a more realistic expectation of the difficulties that they may encounter: the Scottish 2015 study (Norman, 2015a, p. 295) indicated that approximately half of respondents would value support in, for example, 'making plans for the future or in undertaking a transition' (Norman, 2015a, pp. 233, 241). Similarly, thirteen of thirty-three respondents indicated that they would greatly value the support of a suitably qualified social worker because they were no longer receiving GIC input, with a further seven saying that such support would be valued a little – in total, almost two-thirds of respondents. Just two participants said that they would not value this support at all (Table 7.5; Norman, 2015a, p. 295):

A three-way cross-tabulation indicated that four respondents currently living in a male gender role, six in a female gender role (all ten

Table 7.5: The value of advice, information and support from an appropriately trained and experienced social worker or care worker if no longer receiving support/advice with transgender issues from a GIC (Survey one: n = 47).

Valuation of support from a social worker if the respondent is no longer receiving support and advice from a Gender Identity Clinic	Number of respondents	Percentage of respondents
I would value this support greatly	13	40
I would value this support a little	7	21
I don't know if I would value this support	4	12
I would not value this support very much	2	6
I would not value this support at all	2	6
Not applicable: I am still receiving support and advice with transgender issues from a GIC	5	15
Total	**33**	**100**

of whom had a matching gender identity) and two in a transgender role said that they would value this support greatly. These respondents had spent a range of periods in their current gender role, varying from one year, one and a half years, three years, four years (three), six years, eight years, fourteen years, twenty years and twenty-four years (one respondent did not answer this question), suggesting that the need for support was, for a significant proportion, no longer centred around transition issues. Indeed, support during transitioning was only directly relevant to approximately a fifth of these respondents (nine of forty-seven respondents, spread across most age ranges, were currently transitioning, only five of whom were currently receiving GIC support), so the high percentage of those who would value support in the absence of GIC input appears significant (Norman, 2015a, p. 296).

However, the post-transition needs of transgender people receive scant attention in the literature of social care practice: Mallon (2009), Brown and Rounsley (2003) and Brill and Pepper (2008) each include detailed consideration of the issues affecting transition, with much reduced reference to the longer term. However, Morrow and Messinger include a chapter on transgender health issues by Lombardi and Davis but only towards the end of this chapter is there a brief section on 'integration', which includes the suggestion that 'common adjustment challenges in the post-transition period include forming intimate relationships ...

self-acceptance as a non-traditional man or woman ... and coping with stigma in society' (Morrow and Messinger, 2006, p. 359).

Self-acceptance, while more evident post-transition, may be a long-term process for transgender people, particularly those who do not fully self-identify with or who are not readily perceived as belonging to one of the binary gender categories. Lombardi and Davis' notion of coping with stigma in society was touched upon within the previous section relating to social rejection, and is explored further within the following three sections concerning relationships with friends, colleagues and neighbours and with developing a more confident community presence. Their notion of 'intimate relationships' is explored a little within a paragraph on sexual orientation: they note that 'transsexuals span the full range of sexual orientations ... and ... may experience an unexpected change in their sexual orientation during the transition process'. They explain that, as 'sexual orientation depends largely on a stable gender identity, (post-transition transsexuals) may need to explore their new sexual orientation and examine the impact it may have on their relationships', while also suggesting that 'self-acceptance as a non-traditional man or woman' and 'forming (or adjustment within existing) intimate and family relationships' are also important stages in post-transition acclimatisation (Morrow and Messinger, 2006, p. 358).

In addition to seeking to resolve gender dysphoria through gender role reassignment, Coleman *et al.* (1993) suggest that 'transgender individuals go through a second developmental process, for sexual identity'. Hines suggests that post-transition 'transgender sexualities are often fluidly and contingently situated; experiences of gender transition may enable an increased freedom of sexual expression, and offer a greater diversity of sexual identification' (Hines, 2007, p. 125). It may be that such a sense of fluid sexuality in some cases evidences confusion on the part of the transgender person, which may affect the development of new sexual relationships (or even of platonic relationships if confusion or uncertainty over sexuality is apparent to others too) but detailed research into this 'second developmental phase' of post-transition sexual identification is notably lacking.

Relationships with friends

> **Sarah:** 'The real losses I experienced in transition were of
> friendships either immediately upon discovery of my tran-
> sitioning, or after a little while without much explanation'
> (Norman, 2015a, p. 300).

The importance of friends and friendships is mentioned throughout this
book but there is often a sense of duality about the nature of friendship
for the transgender person, which is evident, for example, in the finding
that although almost a third (thirteen of forty) of respondents to the
Scottish (2015) survey rated close friends as of the highest importance
as a source of advice regarding 'helping you to come to terms with your
gender identity' almost as many (ten) considered them as of lowest
importance (Table 1.1). However, the total number of friends rated in
the highest three columns of importance was double the total of those
in the lowest three columns. Similarly, an analysis of the importance
of friendships for support during a transition (Table 3.1) showed that
almost twice as many friends were rated in the three columns of highest importance as in the three columns of lowest importance. It seems
that, if close friendships are in place prior to coming out or transition,
the majority of these friendships may continue to provide a firm basis
of support to the transgender person.

Despite this positive evidence, twelve of twenty-seven participants said
that they would still value assistance from an appropriately trained and
experienced social worker or care worker to help them with relationship
difficulties with their friends linked with being transgender, either greatly
or a little. Just two participants commented that they had not experienced
such difficulties (Table 7.6; Norman, 2015a, p. 301).

A cross-tabulation of this question with age indicated that the numbers of those who would value such assistance greatly tended to rise
gradually with age, up to the age group 46–55, but when those who
would appreciate this assistance a little were included this tended to
even out these age differences almost completely. Five of twelve of
biological males but only one of ten biological females said that support with difficulties with friends would be valued greatly, which might
appear to fit with the conclusion of the NHS/Glasgow survey that
'problems with friendships seem to be greater for MtF respondents

Table 7.6: The value of advice, information and support from an appropriately trained and experienced social worker or care worker to better understand and/or address differences, disagreements or conflicts with friends, concerning being transgender and/or the consequences of transitioning (Survey two: n = 29).

Valuation of support from a social worker if the respondent is no longer receiving support and advice from a Gender Identity Clinic	Number of respondents	Percentage of respondents
I would value this support greatly	13	40
I would value this support a little	7	21
I don't know if I would value this support	4	12
I would not value this support very much	2	6
I would not value this support at all	2	6
Not applicable: I am still receiving support and advice with transgender issues from a GIC	5	15
Total	**33**	**100**

than FtM participants' (Wilson *et al.*, 2005, p. 27). Including those who would value this support a little altered these figures to six of twelve and four of ten respectively.

Twenty-four of twenty-seven respondents were currently receiving no support with difficulties with friendships while twenty-two respondents noted that they had not received such assistance in the past (Norman, 2015a, p. 302).

Relationships with neighbours, colleagues etc.

The NHS/Glasgow University survey found that 'most respondents had experienced verbal aggression (and) threats (and that) there were also many reports of physical aggression' committed by acquaintances, neighbours and strangers' (Wilson *et al.*, 2005, pp. 27–9). On an everyday level, as Brill and Pepper note in regard to transgender children, 'everyone tends to worry about what the neighbours think' suggesting that 'it is up to you to decide whether to tell them and how much information to share. Gossip will spread regardless, as it does in every neighbourhood, about everyone' (Brill and Pepper, 2008, pp. 140–1). Such advice almost certainly applies to transgender people of all ages.

Sharing information is a process that requires some consideration: whether a transgender person starts living in the opposite gender on a chosen date, without letting others around them know beforehand, or whether they take the time to share this information in advance, may significantly affect how some others respond. As one parent of a transgender child quoted in Brill and Pepper explains:

> I started with my most trusted and deepest friends. I eventually sent an announcement letter to our neighbours. Most people have been wonderfully supportive. It's been nearly nine months now, and I have adopted the attitude that if I treat this with shame or embarrassment, I am perpetuating the problem that we have in society (Brill and Pepper, 2008, p. 139).

In relation to workplace colleagues, Brown and Rounsley note that:

> some co-workers are uncomfortable, resistant or even openly hostile … when transsexuals are excluded from meetings and are no longer invited to join their fellow employees for lunch or for social gatherings, it obviously takes an emotional toll.

But they also include examples of supportive written messages from the colleagues of transgender people at the time of transitioning too and note that one 'significant, long-lasting effect of transitioning is that transsexuals are often more productive … because they no longer have to struggle under the … burden of gender dysphoria' (Brown and Rounsley, 2003, pp. 156–8, 163–6) although such a positive outlook may underestimate the long-term effects of post-transition transphobia, social rejection and isolation.

Schilt's study of transmen provides insight into the 'patriarchal dividend' that many of her respondents found themselves receiving as men, including 'more authority, reward and respect in the workplace than they would have received as women, even when they remain in the same job' (Schilt, 2006, p. 465). Her later study of transwomen is quoted by Jeffreys, who notes that 'men who transition lose money, through significant losses in hourly earnings' (Schilt and Wiswall, 2008, p. 4, cited in Jeffreys, 2014, p. 111). A contrasting gradual increase in earnings for FtM people might be reasonably anticipated.

Fourteen of twenty-seven participants within the Scottish 2015 study stated that they would value assistance, greatly or a little, from an appropriately trained and experienced social worker or care worker to help them with relationship difficulties with their colleagues, neighbours and/or acquaintances, linked with being transgender. Seven participants indicated that they did not need such assistance, while three participants said that they had not experienced such difficulties (Table 7.7; Norman, 2015a, p. 304).

Table 7.7: The value of advice, information and support from an appropriately trained and experienced social worker or care worker to better understand and/ or address differences, disagreements or conflicts within relationships with colleagues, neighbours and/or acquaintances, concerning being transgender and/ or the consequences of transitioning (Survey two: n = 29).

Valuation of advice, information and support to help the respondent to address differences with colleagues, neighbours etc.	Number of respondents	Percentage of respondents
I would value this advice, information and support greatly	10	37
I would value this advice, information and support a little	4	15
I don't know how much I would value this advice, information and support	2	7
I would not value this advice, information and support very much	1	4
I would not value this advice, information and support at all	0	0
Not applicable: I do not need this advice, information and support	7	26
Not applicable: I have not experienced such differences, disagreements or conflicts with colleagues, neighbours or acquaintances, linked with being transgender, or transitioning	3	11
Total	**27**	**100**

A cross-tabulation of this question with age indicated that the numbers of those who would value this assistance greatly tended to rise gradually with age up to the age group 46–55, but that when those who would value this assistance a little were included this tended to even out these age differences almost completely. Similarly, the numbers of biological males (six of twelve) and biological females (two of ten) who would value this information greatly were quite different but including those who would value this assistance a little again reduced this difference considerably, increasing the numbers to seven of twelve biological males and five of ten biological females, respectively (Norman, 2015a, pp. 304–5). Twenty-five of twenty-seven participants indicated that they were not receiving such support at present and twenty-three said that they had not received such assistance in the past (Norman, 2015a, p. 305).

Developing a more confident community presence

Transgender people may be at their most vulnerable when they first venture out within their transitioned gender role into their local community. As Brown and Rounsley explain, 'these are the times when they are least likely to pass, as most transsexuals will have just begun taking hormones and ... still exhibit many of the contours and features of their original gender' (Brown and Rounsley, 2003, p. 135). GIC support may be limited and, while some specialist health services (e.g. speech therapy) may assist with aspects of self-presentation, for most transgender people appearing in public for the first time during transition is likely to be a very great step.

However, even for the most practised transitioned transgender person, going out into the local or wider community may continue to involve 'being read' long after the transition period so that 'for many transsexuals it is a daily concern' (Brown and Rounsley, 2003, p. 135). For some, this may involve seeking increasing acceptance within the transitioned gender, without ambiguity. For others, it may lead to a gradual acceptance of, or resignation to, a lifelong transgender status.

Within the Scottish 2015 study, almost a half (twelve of twenty-seven) of participants indicated that they would greatly value assistance from an appropriately trained and experienced social worker or care worker to help them with developing a more confident community presence, with a further three participants saying that they would value this a little. Less than a third (eight) of participants said that they did not need such assistance (Table 7.8; Norman, 2015a, p. 306).

A cross-tabulation of this question with age indicated that the numbers of those who would value assistance with developing a more confident community presence greatly tended to rise steadily with age, up to the age group 46–55, but when those who would value this assistance a little were included this tended to even out these age differences. The

Table 7.8: The value of advice, information and support from an appropriately trained and experienced social worker or care worker to develop a more confident community presence (Survey two: n = 29).

Valuation of advice, information and support to help develop a more confident community presence	Number of respondents	Percentage of respondents
I would value this advice, information and support greatly	12	44
I would value this advice, information and support a little	3	11
I don't know how much I would value this advice, information and support	2	7
I would not value this advice, information and support very much	1	4
I would not value this advice, information and support at all	1	4
Not applicable: I do not need this advice, information and support	8	30
Total	**27**	**100**

numbers of biological males (eight of twelve) and biological females (four of ten) who would value this information either greatly or a little were rather different, suggesting greater need within the former group (Norman, 2015a, p. 306).

In some cases, the lack of a confident community presence appeared to be very debilitating, but just one person said that they were currently receiving support from a social or care worker, one participant indicated that they were receiving this assistance from another source, and two people said that they had received this assistance from a social or care worker in the past. Twenty-three of the twenty-seven participants stated that either they were not receiving such support at present or that they have not received such assistance in the past (Norman, 2015a, pp. 305–6).

Two interviewees' comments reflected on concerns about their future within their community:

> **Amy:** 'I do not like be perceived as a transsexual by society. I did not go through the slow processes of transitioning to become a transsexual … the only issue I think of (that a social worker) could help me with is having loving relationships with males. I must confess that I am frightened about a relationship in case

they get violent with me if I tell them that I'm a transwoman. Also being rejected would hurt me' (Norman, 2015a, p. 307).

Ciaran: 'I sometimes worry about the future children we don't yet have, finding out about me and getting teased ... I would like to move away and start somewhere fresh but for various reasons this is not a viable option' (Norman, 2015a, p. 307).

The notion of community presence has been highlighted by Browne *et al.* (2010), who question 'geography's presumption of man/woman and male/female' (Browne *et al.*, 2010, p. 573). However, Jeffreys' argument against what she perceives as the intrusion of MtF transgender people into women's spaces (including social events, toilets, hospital wards and prisons) suggests that, more than sixty years after the first 'sex changes', and the clarity that legal recognition of transition status has brought, transitioning may yet present unforeseen difficulties, and potentially limited scope for integration and acceptance (Jeffreys, 2014, pp. 163–82). It is not difficult to comprehend the anxiety expressed by some transgender people when they venture out into the local or wider community, given the degree to which the effects of transphobia have been documented: see, for example, Whittle (2000), Hill and Willoughby (2005), Bockting *et al.* (2006), Whittle *et al.* (2007), Stryker and Whittle (2006), Bromley *et al.* (2007), Greenwood and Gruskin (2007), Meyer (2007), Morton (2008), Mitchell and Howarth (2009), Turner *et al.* (2009), Kennedy and Hellen (2010), Roch *et al.* (2010) and McNeil *et al.* (2012).

In view of the potential for difficulties in venturing into the community, the support of a 'buddy' or 'ally' may be valuable. Messinger quotes Washington and Evans (1991, p. 196), who, in relation to LGB people, define an ally as 'a person who is a member of the dominant or majority group who works to end oppression ... through support of, and as an advocate for, the oppressed population' (Messinger, 2006, p. 468). From a transgender perspective, such support might include accompanying and supporting a transgender person into community settings for work, educational or leisure-related activities, and also advising on matters of dress, demeanour etc. at least during the immediate transition period. It is likely, based on Comstock's findings regarding the effect of a companion on reducing violence to gay men and lesbians, that the presence of a male or female ally may reduce discrimination and transphobic behaviour to a transgender person (Comstock, 1992, p. 65). A handful of such allies (which may, of course, include relatives or friends) offering support on a monthly basis each might provide a transgender person with regular weekly supported ventures into the community, greatly assisting in confidence building and integration.

Being accepted and feeling part of a community, part of a family or part of a relationship are likely to involve a continual evolution of self-perception and of perception by others, for those transgender people who transition to live within binary roles, and for those whose sense of ambiguity does not easily fit within the binary:

> **Abigail:** 'I should also say that living as a female is very important to me, and very liberating too, and has healed the appalling feeling I used to have that I didn't somehow really belong to the human race. Recently my daughter had some wonderful news to give me. She said: 'Dad, you're going to be a grandma!' which kind of sums up, very beautifully, how I would like my family to feel about it all. And they mostly do' (Norman, 2015a, p. 305).

CHAPTER 8

The Socialisation of Transgender

Introduction

The relationship between transgender people and society has been an essential theme throughout this book, beginning with the short history of social awareness of transgender and the relationship between social roles and gender/transgender identities (Chapter 1), the provision of dedicated and generic social care services to transgender people (Chapter 2), the social complexity of gender transitions (Chapter 3), concerns about discrimination and transphobia (Chapter 4), transgender-linked social isolation and mental health issues (Chapter 5), family-related matters (Chapter 6) and the social consequences of 'coming out' as transgender within an almost exclusively binary gendered society (Chapter 7).

This, the final chapter of the book, seeks to draw together some of these threads and concludes by proposing how the consequences of socialising transgender might redress the balance of a historically predominantly medical approach to gender dysphoria. The chapter begins with a review of the notions of sex, gender and transgender, in the light of some of the Scottish 2015 study findings, leading to a discussion of the importance of the embodiment of sex and gender. Consideration of the 'erasure' of transgender lives, and reflections on the process of migration, lead to a final consideration of the social care support that forms part of the socialisation of transgender, which is advocated in the book's conclusion.

Reflections on the concepts of sex, gender and transgender

Some of the comments from survey respondents and interviewees of the Scottish 2015 study thoughtfully and perceptively exposed the complexities of sex and gender in relation to what it means to be transgender. The survey participant who explained that their biological sex was female at birth, but that, having subsequently undergone gender reassignment from female to male, he no longer considered it accurate to say that his biological sex was simply female (Norman, 2015a, p. 211) raised a key aspect of gender transition: that it may alter some of the defining aspects of biological sex, reinforcing the presumption of West and Zimmerman's notion of 'sex category' that essential criteria exist and would or should be there (West and Zimmerman, 1987, p. 132). Those who have undergone hormonal or surgical intervention may indeed appear at least to possess such 'essential criteria' for their transitioned gender. In addition, one interviewee suggested that, having been on hormones for some twelve years, the chemical make-up of her body had significantly changed (Norman, 2015a, p. 211): the effects of the regular use of feminising oestrogen in MtF transsexuals and of masculinising testosterone in FtM transsexuals are well documented (Seal, 2007, pp. 157–90), as are the procedures and outcomes of MtF and FtM reassignment surgeries (Barrett, 2007, pp. 201–44 (MtF) and 227–46 (FtM).

Whittle and Turner's interpretation of the Gender Recognition Act 2004 concurs with the notion of sex change alongside gender role reassignment:

> A transsexual person in the UK, on receiving a gender recognition certificate, thus becomes legally not only their 'new' gender, but their sex also now matches this gender, backdated, if desired, to their date of birth (Whittle and Turner, 2007).

However, from the experiences of some research participants, even after transition, the legal basis, the self-perception and the physical alteration of the characteristics of one's gender and biological sex may not necessarily be recognised or confirmed by others enough to be fully accepted socially within one's transitioned gender: visibility may remain a feature of a transgender person's life long after the transition process is completed (Whittle, 2000).

Such visibility, or a failure to pass successfully, may result in an extension of the state of transsexuality contrary to the experience noted by one interviewee, Sarah, who explained that she viewed 'transsexual' as a process that she went through, rather than as an identity in itself (Norman, 2015a, p. 218). It seems that, for some, the transsexual phase may become a long-term or even permanent condition, perhaps replacing a sense of personal isolation prior to transition, with one of societal alienation, outwith the binary, afterwards. In this situation, the notion of West and Zimmerman's distinction between 'sex' and 'sex category' (West and Zimmerman, 1987, p. 132) appears to work to some transgender persons' disadvantage: it seems that they may still be viewed by (some) others as essentially belonging to their original biological sex, either with the assumption that 'essential criteria' do not exist, or that, for those who have undertaken transition, such criteria have been artificially met (particularly so in the case of some more visible MtF transgender people: Whittle, 2000, pp. 49–50).

That visibility may lead to consequential limited social assimilation has been evidenced within the Scottish 2015 study findings. Non-acceptance or failure to pass successfully in a transitioned role sometimes resulted in very punitive responses: Ciaran's experience of verbal and physical abuse (Norman, 2015a, p. 279) and Lucy's description of being spat at, beaten up and refused service in shops (Norman, 2015a, p. 298) are shocking in their severity. There were also examples of less abusive, but nonetheless disabling, responses: for example, where participants lost contact with relatives because of their transgender status, sometimes at the expense of other family relationships. Luke spoke of how his mother found his transition very hard, particularly in view of the rejection from his uncle and aunt, who now ignore him at family gatherings etc. Another interviewee, Sarah, explained that, with the exception of her mother, her family appeared no longer to want to acknowledge her as a family member (Norman, 2015a, pp. 259–60).

Such experiences provide very negative feedback to transgender people, very different from that which almost everyone who grows up in a gender role that matches their gender identity is likely to receive. Nonetheless, there was no suggestion from any of the survey participants or interviewees of the Scottish 2015 study that they felt that they had made a mistake in undertaking a transition to align their gender identity with their gendered behaviour and appearance.

Indeed, one of the striking outcomes of the Scottish 2015 study was the degree to which some participants showed a willingness to carefully consider their status in relation to sex and gender, and to continue reconsidering this as physical and social changes linked with transition became apparent. The clichéd notion that transitioned transgender people adopt very stereotyped binary gender behaviour and appearance may be correct for some, particularly around the transition period, but the Scottish 2015 study indicated a greater flexibility of self-perception within transgender identities (Norman, 2015a, pp. 215–16).

It is the flexibility of these category choices that informs one of the recommendations of this book – the broadening of choice of gender category through the GRC process, which is currently restricted within the binary. The importance of an alternative legal category of transgender needs to be recognised as an alternative to the binary categories, concordant with the recent World Professional Association for Transgender Health (WPATH) statement on Legal Recognition of Gender Identity (Green, 2015).

It is suggested that this transgender category, while following the principles of the 'x' category favoured, for example, in Australia, New Zealand, India and Germany, should be a term that does not reflect the negative or 'absent' connotations that are often associated with 'x' – a short hand symbol mainly used within the UK for marking something as 'wrong', for example. Instead, the term 'transgender' (or intersex for those whose biological sex, rather than their gender identity, does not conform to male or female norms) is preferred, with the initial 'T' (or 'I' for intersex people) being proposed as a bureaucratic shorthand for use in passports etc. The combination T/I could also be used if a shorthand code for both transgender and intersex people is required: but not I/T for obvious reasons.

Embodiment and transgender

Howson highlights the importance of embodiment when she recognises how 'the body is used ... to categorise people into either/or social groups (male/female) that are constituted through and overlaid by social practice and cultural assumptions'. She goes on to argue that, with regard to the binary sex/gender dichotomy, such a 'distinction is now viewed as problematic and unstable' (Howson, 2005, pp. 55, 57), a view that is reinforced through the increasingly recognised categories of intersex and transgender. It seems, however, that for many transgender people changing one's body to at least partially 'match' the sex normally associated with their gender identity becomes a primary objective in the resolution of their gender dysphoria. Ekins and King explain that 'genital surgery often indicate(s) for gender migrants that their journey is over' (Ekins and King, 2006, p. 49). A FtM respondent to the Scottish 2015 study indicated some of the rationale behind surgery when he explained: 'I hope that once my bottom surgery is complete I will feel more comfortable in my own skin' (Norman, 2015a, p. 244). Another FtM respondent noted the importance of other surgical assistance when he explained that 'when I first got my consultation for chest surgery I was told I would probably have to wait about two years ... I was completely devastated' (Norman, 2015a, p. 244).

Surgery and/or hormones may offer the gateway or 'hoops' through which entry to a preferred gendered body is gained, although Connell suggests that 'most (transsexuals) are aware of the limits of bodily change in transition and know the results will not be normative' (Connell, 2012, p. 873). Surgical limitations might be easier to accept by those who perceive themselves as transgender rather than by those whose self-perception is as a man (or woman) trapped in a woman's (or man's) body. In the case of FtM surgery, the limited success of penis construction means that such an acceptance of the likely outcomes of compromised post-surgery embodiment may be essential if 'genital surgery, rather than bringing their body closer to the "norm" in fact makes bodies even more complex and visibly different (serving) to further stigmatise and marginalise these individuals' (Witten and Whittle, 2004, p. 516). Conversely, for MtF migrants, the development of male bodily features, including secondary sexual characteristics such as a male voice and facial structure, during puberty and early adulthood may lead to doubt in others about gender status, in person, by Skype, on the telephone etc., post-transition.

Mitchell and Howarth noted that 'gender reassignment pathways were criticised for a one size fits all approach. Those with more complex or ambiguous gender identities ... may be denied treatment' (Mitchell and Howarth, 2009, p. 62). Thus, even for such non-binary individuals, any expectation within the GIC process that transitioning transsexuals will re-form their bodies to reflect the 'natural' male or female body may be difficult to resist, not least because of continuous exposure to 'perfectly' formed male and female bodies within idealised binary-gendered media advertising: the publicity given to such high-profile transgender women as Caitlin Jenner (*The Guardian*, 2015) and Hari Nef (*The Guardian*, 2016c) is often accompanied by photographs of each of them conforming to an idealised gender appearance and stereotype that few transgender people may be able to afford, or may wish, to mimic.

By initially acknowledging compromise within one's sex and gender status, it may be possible – for some transcending transgender people at least – to choose non-conformity to embodied binary standards too, for as Davidmann suggests: 'contrary to the popular belief that a desire for genital surgery is an essential criteria of a transsexual identity, the focus of transsexual experiences does not always reside with the genitals' (and may present as) 'a counter-narrative to the notion of "being born in the wrong body" '. However, she cautions that while:

> some transsexual people are creating what could be construed as new configurations of sex and gender, the link between trans-sexual well-being and the broader social domain is more significant than is generally acknowledged (Davidmann, 2010, p. 189).

While transgender people may need to be prepared for limitations in flexibility within modern society's attitudes to gender non-conformity, it is nonetheless reasonable to anticipate that individuals, communities and wider society will, over time, gradually accommodate these 'new configurations of sex and gender' so that transgender people become increasingly accepted outwith binary stereotypes of embodiment and gendered behaviour.

Migratory issues

The term 'migration' has been adopted throughout this book (see Glossary of terms), as described by Ekins and King (2006, p. 43) to encapsulate the transition process by which transgender people seek to alter their appearance and gender role to reflect their gender identity. The consideration of gender migration has corresponded with widespread contemporary debate within UK society about economic and social migration, and how this affects both those who live in the country of destination, and migrants themselves.

It is not difficult to find similarities between those who migrate for economic, social or gender-specific reasons: each migrant will leave behind their place of origin and their associated social role within their local community, often involving significant personal loss, with the potential for a distancing or even fracturing of long-established relationships. Each is very likely to carry at least some cultural baggage from their former lives, retained or jettisoned along the way according to the value of such baggage within the new social role, or to the degree to which their former culture can be integrated within their new life. Economic, social and transgender migrants are each likely to have a very significant reason for undertaking such a disruptive journey, ultimately revolving around a need to seek a better and happier life than that which they leave behind. However, the degree to which each is likely to be accepted into their new culture may vary according to the degree to which they are able to adapt and pass successfully within this culture, or to find a subculture that shares their experiences, ideals, hopes and aspirations, and that provides a sense of belonging and a basis for mutually supportive relationships.

Economic and social migrants, whose reasons for migrating may be based on poverty, persecution or war, may nonetheless be viewed as intruders by the citizens of their new country even though their migration does not appear to undermine social systems as fundamental as the permanence of allocated binary gender, which underpins the migration of transgender people. Such responses may mean that they are treated as a threatening and devalued group (consequently accused of taking jobs, houses, health services, school places etc.). This is not dissimilar to the experiences of many transgender migrants, whose presence in both gender-defined spaces (toilets, changing rooms etc.) or even in public spaces that are not gender defined may be seen as unsettling or even threatening to mainstream binary-gendered individuals.

Apparent irrational rejection and stigmatisation of migrants may be based, as Goffman describes, on a 'differentness ... conceptualized collectively by ... society as a whole ... (which) it would be foolish to deny' (Goffman, 1968, p. 149). Thus, for those economic or social migrants who seek integration within British culture, there may be a subtext of difference which, intentionally or not, discourages a sense of belonging to the host culture, leading to the emergence or reinforcement of an ethnic or religious sub-culture for those who share similar points of origin or other mutual characteristics, as a buffer against majority rejection. It is likely no coincidence that an increase in racist and religious hate crime recorded after the British EU referendum in June 2016 also extended to another 'different' culture, through homophobic attacks, which rose by a reported 147% in the three months following the Brexit vote, according to figures compiled by the LGBT anti-violence charity Galop (Lusher, 2016).

Those transgender migrants who do not pass well, and who are perceived as not belonging to the culture of the binary gender to which they have transitioned, may find that this perception of difference intrudes into many aspects of their day-to-day life. Those who seek to transcend binary gender boundaries may find even greater difficulty, as the nature of this difference is still being conceptualised by a largely binary-gendered society, and is likely to be less accepted and understood than binary transition. But, as noted above, as individuals, communities and wider society gradually accept and accommodate new configurations of sex and gender, transgender people should find it easier to live outwith the binary stereotypes to which they are unable to conform. Such individuals, at least in the foreseeable future, may additionally continue to seek a sense of support and commonality within a transgender community, online or within support groups, or take comfort from increasing understanding and acceptance as these develop through wider positive media coverage of transgender issues.

Summary of social care sources and gaps in services

The Scottish 2015 study identified sources and gaps in social care support to transgender people within five key areas of transgender support: (i) transgender support groups; (ii) GICs, GPs; (iii) psychiatrists, counsellors and other health workers; (iv) family, friends and colleagues; and (v) social carers and social workers (see Tables 1.1, 3.1, 5.2, 5.4, 6.2 and 7.1). Social workers and social carers were not rated highly within any of the categories for support, although a separate series of survey questions indicated a consistent need for social care support by respondents across a range of categories (Tables 1.2, 3.2, 5.3, 6.3, 6.4, 7.2, 7.3, 7.4, 7.5, 7.6, 7.7 and 7.8).

Transgender groups have been shown to play a particularly important role in supporting individuals, for they were rated as the most highly valued source of support regarding gender identity and undertaking transition by more than a third of participants (Tables 1.1 and 3.1). Surprisingly, this support was rather more likely to be considered highly by respondents with a male gender role and gender identity than those with a female role/gender identity. Group support was also viewed as being of the highest importance by more than half of respondents for assistance with changing documentation (Table 7.1). However, concerns were raised by both voluntary and statutory sector respondents that group support was not readily available in many parts of Scotland.

It might be anticipated that GIC support would be most appreciated for problems relating to gender identity and undertaking transition. However, such support received very mixed evaluations, with the ratio of respondents rating GIC support within the three categories of highest importance rather than the three categories of lowest importance being approximately 3:2 (Tables 1.1 and 3.1). A tendency was apparent for those with a female role/gender identity to value GIC support more highly than those with a male role/gender identity. A similar polarity of ratings was also noticeable for support with changing documentation, in the ratio of 4:3 (Table 7.1).

Support from counsellors and psychiatrists for gender identity issues also received mixed evaluations, with however, more respondents rating such support within the three categories of highest importance than within the three categories of lowest importance, in a ratio of 3:2 (Table 1.1). The ratio for highest three categories/lowest three categories for undertaking transition was 5:4 (Table 3.1). Transition support from counsellors and psychiatrists tended to be considered of highest importance by those with a female gender role/gender identity, rather than by those with a male role/identity. Counsellors and psychiatrists were also viewed very highly for their support with health problems linked with being transgender by more than a third of respondents (Table 5.4).

GPs were rated most highly by almost half of respondents with more generic, long-term physical or mental health issues, disabilities or problems linked with old age (Table 5.2). Although sixteen people placed GPs in the highest three categories with gender identity issues, thirteen placed them in the lowest three categories (Table 1.1), while the ratio in regard to helping to undertake transition was approximately 5:4 (Table 3.1). Twelve participants placed GPs in the highest three categories with help with changing documentation (perhaps by providing letters confirming the change of gender role), although the same number of participants placed them in the three lowest categories (Table 7.1).

Twenty-five participants rated family members within the highest three categories for support regarding gender identity issues, with a little less than half that number (eleven) placing them in the three lowest categories (Table 1.1). The comparable ratio for help with undertaking transition was 13:11 (Table 3.1). Equal numbers of family members were placed in the three highest and three lowest categories for support with long-term ill health (Table 5.2) and health problems linked with being transgender (Table 5.4).

No clear single source of support to family members was identified: almost equal numbers of participants rated family members in the three highest categories of support as in the lowest three categories of support to other family members regarding gender role transition. Eight participants rated close friends and transgender support groups within the three highest categories for support to family members, with five and two participants respectively placing them within the lowest three categories (Table 6.2).

The ratio of those participants who rated close friends in the three highest categories for support with gender identity issues was more than twice that of those who placed them in the three lowest categories: 24:11 (Table 1.1). The ratio for close friends as a source of support in helping to undertake transition was 21:12 (Table 3.1). Similar numbers of close friends were placed in the three highest and three lowest categories for support with long-term health problems: 11:7 (Table 5.2) as for health problems linked with being transgender: 9:7 (Table 5.4).

Both family members and close friends tended to be rated more highly for support with gender identity issues and undertaking transition by those in a male gender role and with a male gender identity, than by those with a female gender role/identity.

Colleagues and line managers were usually placed in the lowest three categories for support as opposed to the highest three categories, by a ratio of at least 2:1, although more support with documentation changes was noted (Table 7.1).

Social workers and carers were rated poorly by many participants for nearly all the issues of support described above, although some respondents did receive social work/carer support on an individual basis across most categories of need. At least a third of respondents said that they would greatly value advice information and support with:

- gender identity issues (Table 1.2);
- gender role transition (Table 3.2);
- social isolation (Table 5.3);
- support to partners or other family members (Table 6.3);
- support with family conflicts, disagreements or conflicts (Table 6.4);
- changing documentation (Table 7.2);
- applying for a GRC (Table 7.3);
- coping with social rejection and/or abuse (Table 7.4);
- when no longer receiving GIC support (Table 7.5);
- support with conflicts with friends (Table 7.6);
- support with conflicts with colleagues, neighbours and acquaintances (Table 7.7);
- developing a more confident community presence (Table 7.8).

When respondents who said that they would value these types of support 'a little' were included, the overall numbers rose to a half of respondents in most cases, and sometimes to rather more than this fraction (see Tables 5.3, 7.3, 7.4, 7.5 and 7.8 in particular).

Further analysis and comparison of these responses demonstrates moderate, strong or very strong correlations between each of these social care issues for which assistance would be valued, though low respondent numbers prevent statistically significant correlation data from being calculated in all cases. An average of three-quarters of respondents who said that they would greatly value advice on one issue indicated that they would also value advice on other issues (Norman, 2015a, pp. 379–89).

It seems that a small number of available sources of social care support may already be meeting at least some social care needs for some individuals, but that no sources of social concern adequately address such needs for most transgender people. There appears to be a need to improve dedicated social care and support significantly for many transgender people who live within a binary gender or transgender role and/or who undertake transition. It might be anticipated, in the current climate of increasingly financially restricted public services in Scotland, that this is mainly likely to happen when transgender people seek such services from their local providers on an individual basis, rather than by waiting for services to be set up on their behalf.

Self-directed support

Additional opportunities may also exist for transgender people to seek empathetic, personalised social care, for example through self-directed support (SDS), which, while not directly referred to within either the comments of service providers or transgender people within the Scottish 2015 study, is an established and potentially valuable alternative to mainstream social care provision in Scotland.

For more than thirty years the devolution of the provision of social care from statutory authorities to the private and voluntary sectors within the United Kingdom has meant that some social care services, for example care at home and residential care, are now much more likely to be provided privately (but may still be funded by their local authority). SDS might offer a different approach to personalised support to transgender people, though funding for this can be provided only through a statutory authority after initial, detailed financial and needs assessments. SDS offers a number of options for obtaining support, including the provision of a service user's individual budget as a direct payment, which is then used to purchase services 'from a service provider such as a voluntary organisation or care agency, or by employing personal assistants, or a combination of both' (Self-Directed Support Scotland, 2013).

The range of support that may be purchased includes care options to enable a client to continue to live in their own home, 'such as help with having a bath or getting washed and dressed', but it may also be used to assist individuals to take part in activities elsewhere, for example:

> out of the home it could support you to go to college, to continue in employment or take a job, or to enjoy leisure pursuits more ... you might arrange for a personal assistant ... to help you attend local classes, go swimming, or be a volunteer helping others. It could also be used to provide a short break (respite)' (Self-Directed Support Scotland, 2013).

It is not difficult to envisage the potential for a very wide range of personalised assistance, for example, for a socially isolated, lonely or anxious transgender individual, subject to assessment and the availability of financial assistance within the local authority budget.

A further advantage of the SDS Scotland scheme is that the client can opt to set up a contract for support for themselves, rather than leaving this to the funding body, thereby enabling potentially much greater control over both the quality of care and support that they receive, and the way that support staff provide this care and support. Such a self-controlled support scheme may enable transgender people to employ carers who are more likely to be sympathetic to the anomalies and nuances of gender highlighted by transgender status, even if the social care being provided is not transgender related.

Socialising transgender

Hird, in an article on a 'Sociology of transsexualism', concludes that it is 'the possibility of transcending sex and gender altogether that offers, from a sociological perspective, the most interesting possibilities' (Hird, 2002, p. 591). A similar point of view is expressed by McKenna and Kessler, who suggest that transcending gender is 'of greatest importance to gender theorists like us who are interested in the possibility, both theoretical and real, of eliminating gender' (McKenna and Kessler, 2006, p. 349).

Namaste, however, takes a rather more pragmatic perspective:

> transgender discourse is utopian and one profoundly informed by privilege: it assumes that one already has a job, housing and access to health care ... when all of these things are in place, then it is perhaps possible to move through the world in some kind of genderless state, or some state beyond gender (Namaste, 2011, p. 28).

The ubiquity of gender issues that confront transgender people is noted by Abbott, who quotes Jan Morris: 'there seems to be no aspect of existence, no moment of the day, no contact, no arrangement, no response, which is not different for men and women' (Abbott, 2000, p. 140).

The Scottish 2015 study discussed throughout this book has shown that respondents have needed to and have been willing to fundamentally explore their understanding of their own sex and gender, as a way of coming to terms with their sense of identity, of finding a social role that reflects their sense of themselves as quite different from how they had been perceived in the past (Norman, 2015a, pp. 211–21). Each chapter has systematically explored the main areas of need and the current sources of support to transgender people. In addition, the potential additional role of social workers/social carers within statutory and voluntary services has been explored, in assisting transgender people, and in particular migrators and transcenders, with the steps that they need to take in order to find a sense of identity, a social status, a niche in which to live within a community to which they feel they belong.

The gaps in social care noted above, within the support provided during a largely medically monitored transition process, appear to reflect a continuing emphasis on medical perspectives. By this process, the consequences of gender dysphoria have been treated as an illness that is subsequently, to a greater or lesser extent, 'cured' by surgical interventions, often creating a body reflecting as closely as possible that appropriate to an individual's gender identity. An increasing sense of the inadequacy of medical practice to counterbalance the effects of genes and hormones, particularly in the embodiment of transgender people who transition after puberty, has led some to question the role of medicalisation in providing an adequate resolution for gender dysphoria. In addition, Namaste, for example, suggests that 'transsexuals have also objected to a strictly biomedical approach to health at (the gender clinic), one neglecting the important social dimensions of gender transition' (Namaste, 2011, p. 30).

It was noted within the section on Follow-up studies and reviews in Chapter 5 that Pfäfflin and Junge's follow-up review concludes that 'gender reassigning treatments are effective'. However, they also note that 'the results with (FtM people) are, on average, somewhat more favourable than those with (MtF people)' (Pfäfflin and Junge, 1998, pp. 1, 39). Kuiper and Cohen-Kettenis report that 'virtually all FtMs and almost 80% of the MtFs describe integration as good or very good by their own standards' (Kuiper and Cohen-Kettenis, 1988, p. 446), suggesting that more than 20% of MtF people do not describe their integration so positively. Overall, outcomes of follow-up studies suggest that being older, MtF and/or previously heterosexual puts individuals more at risk of loneliness and isolation post-transition, leading to a more likely need for support than those who are younger, FtM and/or previously homosexual.

Dhejne et al.'s recent follow-up study concludes that gender reassignment will still leave some transgender individuals facing 'substantially higher rates of overall mortality, death from cardio-vascular disease and suicide, suicide attempts, and psychiatric hospitalisations ... compared to a healthy control population'. They conclude that 'improved care for the transsexual group after the sex reassignment should therefore be considered' (Dhejne *et al.*, 2011, p. 7). Such studies provide compelling evidence that social care needs to be provided alongside medical care to address and compensate for social factors which may underlie difficulties prior to and during and following transition.

Dietert and Dentice, in an article exploring 'Growing up trans: Socialization and the gender binary', discuss the difficulties within relationships of transgender interviewees as children, with their mothers, fathers and peers, as they sought to express their feelings about their gender, while experiencing 'mainstream social constructions of gender (which) demand conformity by adhering to only two choices of gender identity' (Dietert and Dentice, 2013, p. 24). Some of the findings of the Scottish 2015 study into social care support (in particular those relating to support to transgender people by families and friends, discrimination, transphobia and social isolation) suggest that gender role socialisation in adult transgender people may be similarly difficult and potentially disruptive to these same close relationships, further evidencing the need for targeted advice, support, consideration and understanding within the post-transition adult socialisation process (Norman, 2015a, pp. 250–62).

A further role of social care agencies might also be to promote information sharing and advocacy on a wider scale to develop a greater awareness of the needs of transgender people within society. In addition, as was noted earlier, Burdge argues that it is the responsibility of 'social workers to target society's traditional gender dichotomy for change' (Burdge, 2007, p. 243). By positing more flexible gender roles within society, additional benefits may be apparent for cis-gendered men and women too.

Conclusion

It is proposed that a combination of extended social care support and advocacy on behalf of transgender people is needed to promote a deeper understanding of transgender status, and to provide assistance with the social consequences of transition or transcendence, on both an individual and a societal level. Such an approach needs to supplement and counterbalance the medicalisation of transgender, which has dominated the treatment of gender dysphoria since the middle of the twentieth century. It would not replace medical support, of course, for the need for surgical intervention will remain for migrators who seek embodiment appropriate to their gender identity.

It is also proposed that social care services can offer a valuable advocacy for the establishment of a transgender legal status. This is a natural next step in a society where greater understanding and acceptance of transgender people within individual relationships, communities and wider society are slowly becoming more widespread.

However, until transgender people are more readily accepted as part of a multifaceted society that respects transgender difference alongside differences of sex, gender, sexuality, religion, ethnic origin, disability, nationality etc., it is acknowledged that transgender people will need support prior to, during and beyond transition to a binary or transgender role, through the planning, development and provision of the wide range of additional social care support that has been evidenced by the research findings that underpin this book.

The Scottish 2015 Study

The overall aim of this study was to address the paucity of knowledge about social care service provision to transgender people in Scotland, and to explore the types of services that were available, that were needed and that might be developed to good effect in the future. There were three main objectives:

- clarifying the nature of existing dedicated and generic social care services;
- exploring social care provision, particularly relating to gender identity and gender status;
- addressing social care needs relating to family and friends, work and the wider community.

These three objectives were integrated within the three research questions.

Research Question 1
What types of dedicated/specialist and generic social care services are/ might be requested, made available to or received by transgender people in Scotland, through which statutory and voluntary commissioning and provider organisations, transgender networks and/or individuals seek to meet the assessed and/or perceived needs of transgender people?

Research Question 2
To what extent do/might social care services from the statutory and voluntary sectors assist transgender people in understanding and resolving issues of gender identity and gender status as individuals with binary, transgender, complex or ambiguous gender identities?

Research Question 3
To what extent do/might social care services from the statutory and voluntary sectors assist transgender people with resolving difficulties

within their relationships with family and friends, at work and within their wider communities?

The surveys and interviews

A pilot study was undertaken with a transgender support group based in the north-east of England to trial the questionnaire and to consider the potential value of focus groups within the forthcoming research methodology. Two main methods were subsequently used in the main research with respondents living in Scotland: online surveys and online interviews. Three online surveys were undertaken – two with transgender people and one with service providers/commissioners – offering a range of opportunities to collate both descriptive and analytical data. Nineteen asynchronous, semi-structured online interviews were undertaken to supplement the survey data, with transgender people and service providers/commissioners.

The surveys/interviews of transgender people

In order to reach as many transgender people as possible, it was necessary to target them directly, and to do this the support of the STA was sought. The STA is a voluntary organisation based in Edinburgh but with nationwide connections to individuals and transgender groups in Scotland. They circulated information about the research, and the web address of the initial questionnaire for transgender people, and its subsequent follow-up questionnaire to the individuals and organisations on their mailing lists.

The main section of the first survey was structured around a series of questions that asked about the importance of each of a wide range of potential sources of advice or support, including transgender support groups, family and friends, GPs and GICs, psychiatrists and counsellors, for a range of issues such as 'coming to terms with your gender identity', 'helping you to make (a gender) transition' and 'helping you to change your documentation'.

The sub-themes and themes that formed the basis of the second survey were identified from the data of the first questionnaire and the ten interviews of transgender people, resulting in further important factual information about the different numbers of transgender people who were using, had used or would like to use social care advice and support, and who valued such support, across a wide range of issues.

The main section of the second survey was structured around a repeated series of three separate questions that asked whether advice, information or support from a suitably experienced social worker or care worker would be valued for a range of potential issues such as to help gender identity or transition issues, concerns of family or friends, or to address social isolation, rejection or abuse etc.

Forty-seven questionnaire responses were received for the first survey of transgender people together with twenty-nine questionnaire responses to the second survey of transgender people.

Ten transgender people took part in online interviews by self-selecting to be interviewed at the end of the first survey. These interviews were carried out asynchronously, allowing the participants to consider their responses carefully over several hours (or even days) and to reconsider their initial responses too, offering additional perspectives if they needed to, after further reflection. This period of reflection also allowed the seeking of more detailed information, particularly where an original response had been quite brief.

A focus on 'social care' issues was maintained throughout these semi-structured interviews, basing the questions on the participants' original answers to the preceding questionnaire. An exploration of tangential and background issues was usually avoided, beyond those perspectives already explored within the questionnaire, unless these appeared particularly relevant. However, where interviewees raised issues of concern outwith the immediate perspective of the interviews, these were explored and addressed before returning to the focus of social care.

The transgender research participants consisted in the main of transitioning 'migrators', with only a small number of 'oscillators' and 'transcenders' taking part. It is difficult to conceive of how these two small minorities within what is itself a minority group might have been better represented other than by seeking a larger sampling frame: for example, by including NHS gender clinic patients as well as individuals and groups on the STA mailing list.

Transgender survey attribute data
Attribute data for the respondents to surveys one and two indicated a wide span of ages, home circumstances, employment status, gender identities and gender descriptors, suggesting a broad range of

participants. However, no transgender participants aged under sixteen and only a few transgender people aged 66 or over took part in this research. Their participation would have provided valuable insights and knowledge into the experiences of two age groups at different polarities in their transgender experience. Each of the forty-seven people who took part in survey one was of white origin, suggesting that transgender people from other ethnic groups may not seek or may be unable to access mainstream services, thereby raising a source of concern.

Some 47% of participants of survey one, and 38% of participants of survey two were living alone, compared to 34% of households across Scotland which contain only one person (the percentage of adults living alone across Scotland will, therefore, be rather less than 34%) (Scottish Government, 2013, Section 2).

More than half (twenty-seven of forty-seven) of respondents said that they had already changed their gender role to match their gender identity. Of these twenty-seven individuals thirteen biological males, five biological females and five who described themselves as of 'other' or unspecified biological sex had completed transitions to the (in the main) alternative binary gender role. Some migrators had, however, chosen a non-binary destination: two biological males and one biological female said that they had developed a gender role that reflected a bi-gender identity as both male and female, while one intersex person said that they had developed a gender role to reflect their androgyne gender identity.

In addition, six biological males and three biological females were in the process of transition, and two of each biological sex said that they would like to change their gender role to match their gender identity, giving a total of forty of forty-seven people (85%) who indicated that they fell within a 'migrating' category. Two participants said that they were 'happy to spend some time in the opposite gender role' but did not want to do this permanently.

Biological males outnumbered biological females in the age range 56–65 (by 6:0). Biological females outnumbered biological males in the age group 16–25 (by 6:1) (survey one). Similar ratios were found within survey two. Participants currently in a male role outnumbered those in a female role, within the age groups 16–25 (by 5:2) and 26–35 (by 4:2) (survey one). As might therefore be anticipated, participants in

a female role outnumbered those in a male role within the age groups
36–45 (by 4:2) and 46–55 (by 9:2) (survey one). Similar differences
in the age groups of transgender participants in male or female current
roles were also found in a cross-tabulation of current gender role and
age groups for survey two.

Some 53% (twenty-five) of the forty-seven respondents to survey one
had a degree or postgraduate qualification. The percentage of biological
males (who were more likely to be living in or transitioning to a female
role) with a degree, postgraduate or professional qualification was 36%,
and of biological females (who were more likely to be living in or transitioning to a male role) was 22%. There is little difference between the per-
centages of cis-gendered men and women (27%) with these qualifications
nationally (Scottish Government, 2013: Section 7).

Of the forty-seven participants to survey one who were employed
or self-employed, fourteen (54%) were biological males and five (34%)
were biological females. The figure for women differs significantly from
the national percentage of 49%, though this may reflect the younger
age group of many of the biological females in the survey. The national
percentage figure for men is 58%. Figures for unemployment (five: 9%)
are only a little higher than the national average of 7% (Scottish Government, 2013, Section 5).

Some 24% (thirteen) of forty-seven participants in survey one described
themselves as long-term sick or disabled compared to a national average of
5% who are 'permanently sick or disabled' (Scottish Government, 2013,
Section 5). Almost a third (seven) of the twenty-three people living alone,
and more than a third (eleven) of the thirty-one in the age groups 36–45,
46–55 and 56–65, described themselves as long-term sick or disabled, as
did 20% of biological males and 27% of biological females.

The surveys/interviews of service providers

The survey of service providers was circulated to each member of the
Association of Directors of Social Work (ADSW) Contracts Officers
Group, which has members located in or linked with every local authority in Scotland. They are responsible for liaising with private and voluntary providers of social care support.

The main sections of the survey sought information concerning the
provision of dedicated/specialist local services to transgender adults

and children within the regions of Scotland, both by the service that the participant represented and by other services of which they were aware. The next section of the survey was structured around a series of questions about the accommodation by generic service provision of the needs of transgender adults and children.

The final sections concerned information about full-time equivalent staffing of dedicated/specialist support to transgender people, and the training that both they and generic staff had received in transgender issues or, where applicable, their unmet training needs. Additional questions sought information on policy statements/guidance documents that were in place for the provision of social care services to transgender people within dedicated/specialist and generic service provision, and the client services to which these policy statements and guidance documents referred.

The twelve public sector questionnaire respondents and eight interviewees came from organisations based in twelve of the thirty-two unitary authorities across Scotland. Although mainly focused around the more densely populated central belt, and in particular within Edinburgh and Glasgow, which together account for just over a fifth of the population of Scotland, representation was also included from the north-east, west, south-west and south-east of Scotland.

The eight voluntary-sector questionnaire respondents came from approximately a third (eight of twenty-six) of the organisations on the STA circulation list. These were also based in a range of regions across Scotland, but were mainly focused around the more densely populated central belt.

The semi-structured approach to these online interviews mirrored that used for transgender people, with the inherent flexibility of this approach allowing, for example, the seeking of additional information from new contacts or organisations mentioned by some of the original interviewees. This was particularly important in contacting representatives of, or those liaising with, local service providers.

Limitations in statutory and voluntary responses have inevitably meant that an extensive overview was not possible of dedicated/specialist services across Scotland, resulting in more of a patchwork of knowledge, ideas and experiences than might have been possible if as complete a picture of those services that are available at present had been sought. However, this would almost certainly have meant the pragmatic omission of the research into transgender people's own experiences of such services within this funding and time-limited project.

Data analysis
Data analysis of the survey and interview research findings was influenced by grounded theory, through the identification of sub-themes and themes, and in hypothesising and theorising, prior to, concurrent with and following the main research process. In addition to the main questionnaire data from the transgender surveys, five sets of two-way cross-tabulations were systematically undertaken across all survey responses, by age, biological sex, gender identity, current gender role and home circumstances, together with several additional three-way cross-tabulations, for both surveys one and two. Juxtaposition and alignment of data from each of the surveys with extracts from the interview responses was also an essential part of the data analysis process and the synthesis of the data.

Research Publication
The findings from the study were summarised and considered in the light of other academic research on the subjects covered, within a thesis that was duly submitted to the University of Edinburgh and assessed by Viva, leading to the award of PhD in July 2015. The thesis can be accessed in hard copy and online at the Edinburgh University library (Norman, 2015a).

The research findings were also submitted to the Scottish Government in October 2015, as a summary report with executive summary (Norman, 2015b), which can be downloaded from the STA website (www.scottishtrans.org; accessed 6 December 2016).

Names of participants in the research were restricted to first names within the original thesis, within the report to the Scottish Government and within the account of the research presented in this book: the gender of each participant's presenting first name at the time of the survey was reflected in the substitution of a similarly gendered name in each of these publications.

REFERENCES

Abbott, P. (2000) 'Gender', in Payne, G. (ed.) (2000) *Social Divisions*, London: Macmillan

Adams, T. (2016) 'Transgender children: The parents and doctors on the frontline' (online). Available from URL: www.theguardian.com/society/2016/nov/13/transgender-children-the-parents-and-doctors-on-the-frontline (accessed 22 November 2016)

Addis, S., Davies, M., Greene, G., Macbride-Stuart, S. and Shepherd, M. (2009) 'The health, social care and housing needs of lesbian, gay, bisexual and transgender older people: A review of the literature', *Health and Social Care in the Community*, Vol. 17, No. 6, pp. 647–58

American Psychiatric Association (2013) 'Diagnostic and statistical manual of mental disorders (DSM-5)' (online). Available from URL: www.psychiatry.org/dsm5 (accessed 23 June 2015)

Baron-Cohen, S. (2003) *The Essential Difference: Men, Women and the Extreme Male Brain*, London: Penguin, Allen Lane

Barres, B. (2006) 'Does gender matter?', *Nature*, Vol. 442 (13 July), pp. 133–6

Barrett, J. D. (2007) *Transsexual and Other Disorders of Gender Identity: A Practical Guide to Management*, Abingdon: Radcliffe

Bauer, G. R., Hammond, R., Travers, R., Kaay, M., Hohenadel, K. M. and Boyce, M., (2009) ' "I don't think this is theoretical; This is our lives": How erasure impacts health care for transgender people', *Journal of the Association of Nurses in Aids Care*, Vol. 20, No. 5, pp. 348–61

BBC News Channel (2008) 'Writer Morris "remarries" partner' (online). Available from URL: http://news.bbc.co.uk/1/hi/wales/7434975.stm (accessed 14 January 2015)

Benjamin, H. (1966) *The Transsexual Phenomenon*, New York: The Julian Press

Benvenuto, C. (2012) *Sex Changes*, New York: St Martin's Press

Bern, S. L. (1975) 'Genital knowledge and gender constancy in pre-school children', *Child Development*, Vol. 60, pp. 649–62

Biblarz, T. J. and Savci, E. (2010) 'Lesbian, gay, bisexual and transgender families', *Journal of Marriage and Family*, Vol. 72, No. 3, pp. 480–97

Billings, D. B. and Urban, T. (1996) 'Socio-medical construction of transsexualism' in Ekins, R. and King, D. (1996) *Blending Genders Social Aspects of Cross-Dressing and Sex-Changing*, London: Routledge

Bockting, W. O., Knudson, G. and Goldberg, J. M. (2006) 'Counselling and mental health care for transgender adults and loved ones', *International Journal of Transgenderism*, Vol. 9, Nos 3–4, pp. 35–103

Bolin, A. (1996) 'Transcending and transgendering: Male-to-female transsexuals, dichotomy and diversity', in Herdt, G. (ed.) (1996) *Third Sex, Third Gender:*

Beyond Sexual Dimorphism in Culture and History, New York: Zone

Bradley, H. (1996) *Fractured Identities*, Cambridge: Polity

Bradley, H. (2007) *Gender*, Cambridge: Polity

Brill, S. and Pepper, R. (2008) *The Transgender Child: A Handbook for Families and Professionals*, San Francisco: Cleis

Bromley, C., Curtice, J. and Given, L. (2007) 'Scottish social attitudes survey: Main findings' (online). Available from URL: www.scotland.gov.uk/Publications/2007/12/04093547/1 (accessed 19 February 2013)

Brown, M. L. and Rounsley, C. A. (2003) *True Selves: Understanding Transsexualism for Families, Friends, Co-Workers and Helping Professionals*, San Francisco: Wiley

Brown, N. (2007) 'Stories from outside the frame: Intimate partner abuse in sexual-minority women's relationships with transsexual men', *Feminism and Psychology*, Vol. 17, No. 3, pp. 373–93

Browne, K., Nash, C. and Hines, S. (2010) 'Towards trans geographies', *Gender, Place and Culture*, Vol. 17, No. 5, pp. 573–7

Burdge, B. J. (2007) 'Bending gender, ending gender: Theoretical foundations for social work practice with the transgender community', *Social Work*, Vol. 52, No. 3, pp. 243–50

Butler, J. (1990) *Gender Trouble: Feminism and the subversion of identity*, London, Routledge

Butler, J. (1993) *Bodies That Matter: On the Discursive Limits of Sex*, New York, Routledge

Byne, W. (2006) 'Developmental endocrine influences on gender identity: Implications for management of disorders of sex development', *Mt Sinai Journal of Medicine*, Vol. 73, No. 7, pp. 950–9

Byne, W. (2007) 'Biology and sexual minority status', in Meyer, I. and Northridge, M. (eds) (2007) *The Health of Sexual Minorities. Public Health Perspectives on Lesbian, Gay, Bisexual and Transgender Populations*, New York: Springerlink

Cartwright, C.M., Hughes, M. and Lienert, T (2012), 'End-of-life care for gay, lesbian, bisexual and transgender people', *Culture, Health & Sexuality: An International Journal for Research, Intervention and Care*, vol. 14, no. 5, pp. 537–548.

Channel Four (2011) 'My transsexual summer' (online). Available from URL: www.channel4.com/programmes/my-transsexual-summer/4od (accessed 27 February 2013)

Channel Four (2016) 'Kids on the edge: The gender clinic'. Available from URL: www.channel4.com/programmes/kids-on-the-edge/on-demand/59713–001 (accessed 22 November 2016

Cohen, H. L., Padilla, Y. C. and Aravana, V. C. (2006) 'Psychosocial support for families of gay, lesbian, bisexual and transgender people', in Morrow, D. F. and Messinger, L. (2006) *Sexual Orientation and Gender Expression in Social Work Practice*, New York: Columbia University Press

Cohen-Kettenis, P. T. and van Goozen, S. H. M. (1997) 'Sex reassignment of adolescent transsexuals: Follow-up study', *Journal of the American Academy of Child and Adolescent Psychology*, Vol. 36, No. 2, pp. 263–71

Coleman, E., Bockting, W. and Gooren, L. (1993) 'Homosexual and bisexual identity in sex-reassigned female to male transsexuals', *Archives of Sexual Behaviour*, Vol. 22, No. 1, pp. 37–50

Comstock, G. D. (1992) *Violence Against Lesbians and Gay Men*, Columbia: Columbia University Press

Concannon, L. (2009) 'Developing inclusive health and social care policies for older LGBT citizens', *British Journal of Social Work*, Vol. 39, No. 3, pp. 403–17

Connell, R. (2009) *Gender: In World Perspective*, Cambridge: Polity

Connell, R. (2010) 'Two cans of paint: A transsexual life story, with reflections on gender change and history', *Sexualities*, Vol. 13, No. 1, pp. 3–19

Connell, R. (2012) 'Transsexual women and feminist thought: Towards new understanding and new politics, *Signs*, Vol. 37, No. 4, pp. 857–81

Cox, L. (2014) 'Laverne Cox flawlessly shuts down Katie Couric's invasive questions about transgender people' (online). Available from URL: www.salon.com/2014/01/07/laverne_cox_artfully_shuts_down_katie_courics_invasive_questions_about_transgender_people (accessed 30 November 2015)

Cruz, T. M. *(2014)* 'Assessing access to care for transgender and gender nonconforming people: A consideration of diversity in combating discrimination', *Social Science and Medicine*, Vol. 110, p. 65

Daly, M. (1978) 'Gyn/Ecology: The meta-ethics of radical feminism', Boston, MA: Beacon Press, cited in Connell, R. (2012) 'Transsexual women and feminist thought: Towards new understanding and new politics, *Signs*, Vol. 37, No. 4, pp. 857–81

Davidmann, S. (2010) 'Beyond borders: Lived experiences of atypically gendered transsexual people', in Hines, S. and Sanger, T. (2010) *Transgender Identities: Towards a Social Analysis of Gender Diversity*, London: Routledge

Davidson, M. (2007) 'Seeking refuge under the umbrella: Inclusion, exclusion, and organizing within the category Transgender (*sic*)', *Sexuality Research and Social Policy*, Vol. 4, No. 4, pp. 60–80

Davies, B. (2002) 'Becoming male or female', in Jackson, S. and Scott, S. (eds) (2002) *Gender: A Sociological Reader*, London: Routledge

Davis, C. (2009) 'Introduction to practice with transgender and gender variant youth', in Mallon, GP (ed.) (2009) *Social Work Practice with Transgender and Gender Variant Youth*, Abingdon: Routledge

Davis, E. C. (2002) 'Negotiating gender and sexual boundaries: Examining how intimate partners make sense of gender transitions', paper to the American Sociological Association, Chicago

De Beauvoir, S. (1949, reprinted 1972) *The Second Sex*, Aylesbury: Penguin

De Cuypere, G., Elaut, E., Heylens, G., Van Maele, G., Selvaggi, G., T'Sjoen, G., Rubens, R., Hoebeke, P. and Monstrey, S. (2006) 'Long-term follow-up: Psychosocial outcome of Belgian transsexuals after sex reassignment surgery', *Sexologies*, Vol. 15, pp. 126–33

Dhejne, C, Lichtenstein, P, Boman, M, Johansson, A. L. V. and Långström, N. (2011) 'Long-term follow-up of transsexual persons undergoing sex reassignment surgery: Cohort study in Sweden', *PLoS ONE*, Vol. 6, No. 2, pp. 1–8

Diamond, M. and Sigmundson, H. K. (1997a) 'Sex reassignment at birth: A long term review and clinical implications', *Archives of Pediatric and Adolescent Medicine*, Vol. 150, pp. 298–304

Diamond, M. and Sigmundson, H. K. (1997b) 'Management of intersexuality: Guidelines for dealing with persons with ambiguous genitalia', *Archives of Pediatrics and Adolescent Medicine*, Vol. 151, pp. 1046–50

Dietert, M. and Dentice, D. (2013) 'Growing up trans: Socialization and the gender binary', *Journal of GLBT Family Studies*, Vol. 9, No. 1, pp. 24–42

Doan, P. L. (2010) 'The tyranny of gendered spaces – reflections from beyond the gender dichotomy', *Gender, Place and Culture*, Vol. 17, No. 5, pp. 635–54

Dreger, A. D. (1998) *Hermaphrodites and the Medical Intervention of Sex*, Cambridge, MA: Harvard University Press

Ekins, R. and King, D. (2006) *The Transgender Phenomenon (sic)*, London: Sage

Erhardt, V. (ed.) (2007) *Head Over Heels; Wives Who Stay with Cross-Dressers and Transsexuals*, New York, NY: Routledge

Fausto-Sterling, A. (1992) *Myths of Gender: Biological Theories about Women and Men*, 2nd edn, New York, NY: Basic Books

Fine, C. (2010) *Delusions of Gender: The Real Science Behind Sex Differences*, London: Icon

Formby, E. (2012) 'Solidarity but not similarity? LGBT communities in the twenty first century' (online), Sheffield Hallam University. Available from URL: http://shura.shu.ac.uk/6528/1/LGBT_communities_final_report_Nov2012.pdf (accessed 5 March 2013)

GIRES (2015a) 'Individual help' (online). Available from URL: www.gires.org.uk/whatwedo (accessed 14 December 2015)

GIRES (2015b) 'Monitoring gender nonconformity – A quick guide' (online). Available from URL: www.gires.org.uk/assets/Workplace/Monitoring.pdf (accessed 14 December 2015)

GLAAD (2014) 'Transgender day of remembrance' (online). Available from URL: www.glaad.org/tdor?gclid=CJeFrMun6MECFSuWtAod-nwAIQ (accessed 7 November 2014)

Goffman, E. (1968) *Stigma*, London: Pelican

Green, J. (2015) 'WPATH statement on legal recognition of gender identity' (online). Available from URL: http://tgeu.org/wpath-2015-statement-on-gender-identity-recognition (accessed 19 December 2016)

Greenwood, G. L. and Gruskin, E. P. (2007) 'LGBT tobacco and alcohol disparities', in Meyer, I. and Northridge, M. (eds) (2007) *The Health of Sexual Minorities. Public Health Perspectives on Lesbian, Gay, Bisexual and Transgender Populations*, New York: Springerlink

Greer, G. (1999) *The Whole Woman*, London: Doubleday

Greer, G. (2015) 'Germaine Greer defends "grossly offensive" comments about transgender women: "Just because you lop off your d**k doesn't make you a ******* woman" ' (online), *Independent on Line. Available from URL:* www.independent.co.uk/news/people/germaine-greer-defends-grossly-offensive-comments-about-transgender-women-just-because-you-lop-off-a6709061.html (accessed 26 November 2015)

Guardian, The (2015) 'Kim Kardashian may have broken the internet, but Caitlyn Jenner united it' (online). Available from URL: www.theguardian.com/fashion/2015/jun/02/caitlyn-jenner-vanity-fair-cover-kim-kardashian-unites-acceptance-transgender-issues (accessed 16 August 2016)

Guardian, The (2016a) 'Gender identity clinic services under strain as referral rates soar' (online). Available from URL: www.theguardian.com/society/2016/jul/10/transgender-clinic-waiting-times-patient-numbers-soar-gender-identity-services (accessed 19 July 2016)

Guardian, The (2016b) 'Navy sailor charged in death of black transgender woman in Mississippi' (online). Available from URL: www.theguardian.com/us-news/2016/jul/26/dee-whigham-black-transgender-woman-killed-us-navy (accessed 1 August 2016)

Guardian, The (2016c) 'Meet Hari Nef: Actor, model – and Elle's first transgender cover girl in UK' (online). Available from URL: www.theguardian.com/society/2016/jul/30/hari-nef-changing-world-transgender (accessed 16 Augusts 2016)

Hare, L., Bernard, P., Sánchez, F. J., Baird, P. N., Vilain, E., Kennedy, T. and Harley, V. (2009) 'Androgen receptor repeat length polymorphism associated with male-to-female transsexualism', Biological Psychiatry, Vol. 65, No. 1, pp. 93–6

Harper, C. (2007) Intersex, Oxford/New York, NY: Berg

Hastings, D. W. (1974) 'Postsurgical adjustment of male transsexual patients', Plastic Surgery, Vol. 1, pp. 335–44

Hellen, M. (2009) 'Transgendered children in school', Liminalis. Available from URL: http://eprints.gold.ac.uk/3531/1/Liminalis-2009-Hellen.pdf (accessed 21 February 2013)

Herdt, G. (ed.) (1996) Third Sex, Third Gender: Beyond Sexual Dimorphism in Culture and History, New York, NY: Zone

Hill, D. and Willoughby, B. (2005) 'The development and validation of the genderism and transphobia scale', Sex Roles, Vol. 53, No. 7, pp. 531–44

Hines, S. (2007) Transgendering care: Practices of care within transgender communities, Critical Social Policy, 27, 4, 462–486

Hird, M. J. (2002) 'For a sociology of transsexualism'. Sociology, Vol. 36, pp. 577–95

Hoff Sommers, C. (1994) Who Stole Feminism – How Women Have Betrayed Women, New York: Simon and Schuster

Hoff Sommers, C. (2013) The War Against Boys – How Misguided Policies Are Harming Our Young Men, New York: Simon and Schuster

House of Commons Women's and Equalities Committee (2016) 'Transgender equality: First report of session 2015–16' (online). Available from URL: www.publications.parliament.uk/pa/cm201516/cmselect/cmwomeq/390/39002.htm (accessed 6 December 2016)

Howson, A. (2005) Embodying Gender, London: Sage

Intons-Peterson, M. (1988) Children's Concepts of Gender, Norwood, NJ: Ablex

Jacklin, C. N. (1989) 'Female and male: Issues of gender', American Psychologist, Vol. 44, No. 2, pp. 127–33

Jeffreys, S. (2014) Gender Hurts, Abingdon: Routledge

Kenagy, G. P. (2005) 'Transgender health: Findings from two needs assessment studies in Philadelphia', Health and Social Work, Vol. 30, No. 1, pp. 19–26

Kennedy, N. and Hellen, M. (2010) 'Transgender children: More than a theoretical challenge, Graduate Journal of Social Science, Vol. 7, No. 2, pp. 25–43

Kessler, S. (1990) 'The medical construction of gender: Case management of intersexed infants', Signs: The Journal of Women in Culture and Society, Vol. 16, pp. 3–26

Kessler, S. J. and McKenna, W. (1978) Gender, An Ethnomethodological Approach, Chicago, IL: John Wiley & Sons and University of Chicago Press

Khosla, D. (2006) *Both Sides Now, One Man's Journey Through Womanhood,* New York, NY: Penguin

Kimura, D. (1999) 'Sex differences in the brain', *Scientific American,* Spring, p. 27

King, D. (1996) 'Cross-dressing, sex-changing and the press', in Ekins, R. and King, D. (1996) *Blending Genders Social Aspects of Cross-Dressing and Sex-Changing,* London: Routledge

Kuiper, A. J. (1991) *Transsexualism, An Evaluation of Sex Reassignment,* Utrecht: Elinhwijk

Kuiper, B. and Cohen-Kettenis, P. (1988) 'Sex reassignment surgery: A Study of 141 Dutch transsexuals', *Archives of Sexual Behaviour,* Vol. 17, No. 5, pp. 439–57

Ladin, J. (2012) *Through the Door of Life, A Jewish Journey Between Genders,* Madison, WI: University of Wisconsin Press

Lawrence, A. A. (2007) 'Transgender health concerns', in Meyer, I. and Northridge, M. (eds) (2007) *The Health of Sexual Minorities: Public Health Perspectives on Lesbian, Gay, Bisexual and Transgender Populations,* New York, NY: Springerlink

Lev, A. I. (2006) 'Transgender emergence within families', in Morrow, D. F. and Messinger, L. (2006) *Sexual Orientation and Gender Expression in Social Work Practice,* New York, NY: Columbia University Press

Lombardi, E. and Davis, S. M. (2006) 'Transgender health issues', in Morrow, D. F. and Messinger, L. (2006) *Sexual Orientation and Gender Expression in Social Work Practice,* New York, NY: Columbia University Press

Lusher, A. (2016) 'Homophobic attacks rose 147 per cent after the Brexit vote', *The Independent* (online). Available from URL: www.independent.co.uk/news/uk/home-news/brexit-hate-crime-hatred-homophobia-lgbt-147-per-cent-rise-double-attacks-on-gays-lesbians-a7352411.html (accessed 21 October 2016)

Maccoby, E. E. and Jacklin, C. N. (1974) *The Psychology of Sex Differences,* Stanford, CA:, Stanford University Press

McKenna, W. and Kessler, S. J. (2006) 'Transgendering: Blurring the boundaries of gender', in Evans, M., Davis, K. and Lorber, J. (eds) (2006) *Handbook of Gender and Women's Studies,* Thousand Oaks, CA: Sage

McNeil, J., Bailey, L., Ellis, S., Morton, J. and Regan, M. (2012) 'Trans mental health and emotional wellbeing study', Scottish Transgender Alliance/Sheffield Hallam University. Available from URL: www.scottishtrans.org/Uploads/Resources/trans_mh_study.pdf (accessed 26 February 2013)

Mallon, G. P. (ed.) (2009) *Social Work Practice with Transgender and Gender Variant Youth,* Abingdon: Routledge

Mallon, G. P. and DeCrescenzo, T. (2009) 'Social work practice with transgender and gender variant children and youth', in Mallon, GP (ed.) (2009) *Social Work Practice with Transgender and Gender Variant Youth,* Abingdon: Routledge

Meadow, T. (2010) 'A rose is a rose: On producing legal gender classifications', *Gender and Society,* Vol. 24, pp. 814–37

Mercer, D. (2014) 'More transgender hate-crime victims', *Independent i,* 27.12.14

Messinger, L. (2006) 'Towards affirmative practice', in Morrow, D. F. and Messinger, L. (2006) *Sexual Orientation and Gender Expression in Social Work Practice,* New York, NY: Columbia University Press

Meyer, I. (2007) 'Prejudice and discrimination as social stressors', in Meyer, I. and

Northridge, M. (eds) (2007) *The Health of Sexual Minorities: Public Health Perspectives on Lesbian, Gay, Bisexual and Transgender Populations*, New York, NY: Springerlink

Meyer, J. K. and Hoopes, J. E. (1974) 'The gender dysphoria syndromes: A position statement on so-called transsexualism', *Plastic and Reconstructive Surgery*, Vol. 54, pp. 444–51

Meyerowitz, J. (2002) *How Sex Changed: A History of Transsexuality in the United States*, Cambridge, MA : Harvard University Press

Meyerowitz, J. (2006) 'A 'fierce and demanding' drive', in Stryker, S. and Whittle, S. (2006) *'The Transgender Studies Reader'*, New York, NY: Routledge

Mind (2013) 'LBGTQ mental health' (online). Available from URL: www.mind.org.uk/information-support/guides-to-support-and-services/sexuality-and-mental-health (accessed 14 April 2014)

Mitchell, M. and Howarth, C. (2009) *Trans Research Review*, Manchester: National Centre for Social Research, Equality and Human Rights Commission,

Money, J. (1994) 'The concept of gender identity disorder in childhood and adolescence after 39 years', *Journal of Sex and Marital Therapy*, Vol. 20, pp. 163–77

Money, J. and Tucker, P. (1976) *Sexual Signatures: On Being a Man or a Woman*, London: Harrap

Morgan, L. and Bell, N. (2003) *First Out … Report of the Findings of the Beyond Barriers Survey of Lesbian, Gay, Bisexual and Transgender People in Scotland*, Stonewall: Beyond Barriers. Available from URL: www.stonewall.org.uk/documents/First_Out_PDF_Report.pdf (accessed 5 March 2013)

Morris, J. (1974) *Conundrum*, London: Faber and Faber

Morris, M. (2007) 'Psychotherapy for gender disorders', in Barrett, J. D. (2007) *Transsexual and Other Disorders of Gender Identity: A Practical Guide to Management*, Abingdon: Radcliffe

Morrow, D. F. (2004) 'Social work practice with gay, lesbian, bisexual, and transgender adolescents', *Families in Society*, Vol. 85, No. 1, pp. 91–9

Morrow, D. F. and Messinger, L. (2006) *Sexual Orientation and Gender Expression in Social Work Practice*, New York, NY: Columbia University Press

Morton, J. (2008) *Transgender Experiences in Scotland*, Scottish Transgender Alliance. Available from URL: http://www.scottishtrans.org/wp-content/uploads/2013/03/staexperiencessummary03082.pdf (accessed 19 February 2013)

Murgatroyd, S. and Woolfe, R. (1985) *Helping Families in Distress: An Introduction to Family Focused Helping*, London: Open University Press

Namaste, V. (2006) 'Genderbashing: Sexuality, gender and the regulation of public space', in Stryker, S. and Whittle, S. *The Transgender Studies Reader*, New York, NY: Routledge

Namaste, V. (2011) *Sex Change, Social Change*, second edn, Toronto, Women's Press

Norman, K. (2015a) ' "Socialising transgender", social care and transgender people in Scotland: A review of statutory and voluntary services and other transgender experiences of social care support', PhD thesis, available from University of Edinburgh Library

Norman, K. (2015b) '"Socialising transgender", social care and transgender people in Scotland: A review of statutory and voluntary services and other transgender experiences of social care support', a report to the Scottish Government. Available from URL: www.scottishtrans.org/resources (accessed 30 September 2016)

Ormston, R., Curtice, J., McConville, S. and Reid, S. (2011) 'Scottish social attitudes 2010: Attitudes to discrimination and positive action' (online). Available from URL: www.gov.scot/resource/doc/355716/0120166.pdf (accessed 3 October 2015)

Pepper, R. (2012) *Transitions of the Heart. Stories of Love, Struggle and Acceptance by Mothers of Gender Variant Children*, Berkeley, CA: Cleis Press

Pfäfflin, F. and Junge, A. (1998) *Sex Reassignment. Thirty Years of International Follow-Up Studies After Sex Reassignment Surgery: A Comprehensive Review, 1961–1991*, IJT Electronic Books. Available from URL: www.symposion.com/ijt/pfaefflin/1000 (accessed 10 March 2015)

Pringle, R. (1992) 'Absolute sex? Unpacking the sexuality/gender relationship', in Connell, R. and Dowsett, G. W. (eds) (1992) *Rethinking Sex: Social Theory and Sexuality Research*, Melbourne: Melbourne University Press

Prosser, J. (1998) *Second Skins, The Body Narratives of Transsexuality,* New York, NY: Columbia University Press

Raymond, J. G. (1980) *The Transsexual Empire,* London: Women's Press

Reddit (2016) 'The /r/transpassing community, or: How I learned to stop worrying and love the report button' (online). Available from URL: www.reddit.com/r/transpassing (accessed 16 August 2016)

Reed, B., Rhodes, S., Schofield, P. and Wylie, K. (2009) *Gender Variance in the UK: Prevalence, Incidence, Growth and Geographic Distribution*, Ashtead, Surrey: Gender Identity Research and Education Society (GIRES)

Richardson, D. (2008) 'Conceptualising gender', in Richardson, D. and Robinson, V. (2008) *Introducing Gender and Women's Studies*, 3rd edn, Basingstoke/New York, NY: Palgrave

Roch, A., Morton, J. and Ritchie, G. (2010) 'Out of sight, out of mind: Transgender people's experiences of domestic abuse', LGBT Domestic Abuse Project, Scottish Transgender Alliance. Available from URL: www.scottishtrans.org/Uploads/Resources/trans_domestic_abuse.pdf (accessed 19 February 2012)

Rogers, A. (2015) Now Russia Makes Transgender Driving a Criminal Offence *Independent* 09.01.15 http://www.independent.co.uk/news/world/europe/now-russia-makes-transgender-driving-a-criminal-offence-9969169.html

Rosser, B. R. S., Oakes, J. M., Bockting, W. O. and Miner, M, (2007) 'Capturing the social demographics of hidden sexual minorities: An internet study of the transgender population in the United States', *Sexuality Research and Social Policy*, Vol. 4, No. 2, pp. 50–64

Rubin, G. (1975) 'The traffic in women: Notes on the "political economy" of sex', in Nicholson, L. (ed.) (1975) *The Second Wave: A Reader in Feminist Theory*, New York, NY/London: Routledge, 1997), pp. 27–62

Ryan, C., Russell, S. T., Huebner, D., Diaz, R. and Sanchez, J. (2010) 'Family acceptance in adolescence and the health of LGBT young adults', *Journal of Child and Adolescent Psychiatric Nursing, Vol.* 23, No. 4, pp. 205–13

Schilt, K. (2006) 'Just one of the guys? How transmen make gender visible at work', *Gender & Society,* Vol. 20, No. 4, pp. 465–90

Schilt, K. and Westbrook, L. (2009) 'Doing gender, doing heteronormativity: "Gender normals, transgender people, and the social maintenance of heterosexuality" ', *Gender and Society,* Vol. 23, No. 4, pp. 440–64

Schilt, K. and Wiswall, M. (2008) 'Before and after: Gender transitions, human capital and workplace experiences', *The B. E. journal of Economic Analysis and Policy, Vol.* 8, No. 1, pp. 1–28

Scottish Government (2013) 'Scottish household survey: Scotland's people annual report: Results from 2012' (online). Available from URL: http://www.gov.scot/Resource/0043/00432400.pdf (accessed 6 December 2016)

Scottish Government (2016) 'Scottish social attitudes 2015: Attitudes to discrimination and positive action' (online). Available from URL: www.ssa.natcen.ac.uk/media/38903/attitudes-to-discrimination-and-positive-action-2015.pdf (accessed 3 October 2016)

Seal, L. J. (2007) 'The practical management of hormonal treatment in adults with gender dysphoria', in Barrett, J. D. (2007) *Transsexual and Other Disorders of Gender Identity: A Practical Guide to Management,* Abingdon, Radcliffe

Self-Directed Support Scotland (2013). 'What is self-directed support?' (online). Available from URL: www.selfdirectedsupportscotland.org.uk/directing-your-own-support http://www.selfdirectedsupportscotland.org.uk (accessed 19 December 2016)

Siverskog, A. (2014) ' "They just don't have a clue: Transgender aging and implications for social work', *Journal of Gerontological Social Work, Vol.* 57, Nos 2–4, pp. 386–406

Smith, P. K. and Cowie, H. (1991) *Understanding Children's Development,* 2nd edn, Oxford: Blackwell

Stanley, L. and Wise, S. (2002) 'What's wrong with socialisation?', in Jackson, S. and Scott, S. (eds) (2002) *Gender: A Sociological Reader,* London: Routledge

Stonewall (2015) 'Briefing papers and publications of the sexual orientation and gender identity advisory group' (online). Available from URL: http://www.stonewall.org.uk/our-work/stonewall-research (accessed 19 December 2016)

Stotzer, R. L., Silverschanz, P. and Wilson, A. *(2013)* 'Gender identity and social services: Barriers to care', *Journal of Social Service Research, Vol. 39, No. 1, pp. 63–77*

Stryker, S. (2008) *Transgender History,* Berkeley, CA: Seal

Stryker, S. and Whittle, S. (2006) *The Transgender Studies Reader,* New York, NY: Routledge

Taylor, E. T. (2013) 'Transmen's health care experiences: Ethical social work practice beyond the binary', *Journal of Gay and Lesbian Social Services,* Vol. 25, No. 1, pp. 102–20

Tolley, C. and Ranzijn, R. (2006) 'Heteronormativity amongst staff of residential aged care facilities', *Gay and Lesbian Issues and Psychology Review,* Vol. 2, No. 2, pp. 78–86

Turner, L., Whittle, S. and Combs, R. (2009) *Transphobic Hate Crime in the European Union,* Press For Change. Available from URL: http://www.ilga-europe.org/sites/default/files/transphobic_hate_crime_in_the_european_union_0.pdf (accessed 19 December 2016)

United Kingdom Government (2004) 'The Gender Recognition Act and Equal

Treatment Directive' (online). Available from URL: www.legislation.gov.uk/ukpga/2004/7/contents (accessed 4 March 2012)

Washington, J. and Evans, N. J. (1991) 'Becoming an ally', in Evans, N. J. and Wall, V. A. (eds) (1991) *Beyond Tolerance: Gays, Lesbians and Bisexuals on Campus*, Alexandria, VA: American College Personnel Association, quoted in Morrow, D. F. and Messinger, L. (2006) *Sexual Orientation and Gender Expression in Social Work Practice*, New York, NY: Columbia University Press

West, C. and Zimmerman, D. (1987) 'Doing gender', *Gender and Society*, Vol. 2, pp. 125–51

Whittle, S. (1996) 'Gender fucking or fucking gender?', in Ekins, R. and King, D. (1996) *Blending Genders Social Aspects of Cross-Dressing and Sex-Changing*, London: Routledge

Whittle, S. (2000) *The Transgender Debate*, Reading: Garnet Publishing

Whittle, S. (2008) 'Name changing on personal documents: A guide for organisations', Press for Change. Available from URL: https://uktrans.info/attachments/article/157/NameChanges.pdf (accessed 19 December 2016)

Whittle, S. and Turner, L. (2007) ' "Sex changes: Paradigm shifts in "sex" and "gender" following the Gender Recognition Act, *Sociological Research Online*. Vol. 12, No. 1

Whittle, S., Turner, L., Al-Alami, M., Rundall, E. and Thom, B. (2007) 'Engendered Penalties: Transgender and transsexual people's experiences of inequalities and discrimination: The Equalities Review', Press for Change and Manchester Metropolitan University. Available from URL: www.pfc.org.uk/pdf/EngenderedPenalties.pdf (accessed 19 February 2013)

Willis, P., Ward, N. and Fish, J. (2011) 'Searching for LGBT carers: Mapping a research agenda in social work and social care', *British Journal of Social Work*, Vol. 41, pp. 1304–20

Wilson, P., Sharpe, C. and Carr, S. (1999) 'The prevalence of gender dysphoria in Scotland', *British Journal of General Practice*, Vol. 49, No. 449, pp. 991–2

Wilson, P., Carr, S., Young, R., Fleming, P., Speirs, A. and McConnachie A. (2005) 'NHS/Glasgow University: Scottish transgender survey – final report' (online). Available from URL: www.nes.scot.nhs.uk/nes_resources/lgbt/documents/6%20Training_activities_resources/6%20Trans_awareness/Resources/Trans_Survey_Glasgow_Uni.pdf (accessed 1 March 2013)

Winterson, J. (2011) *Why Be Happy When You Could Be Normal?*, London: Jonathan Cape

Witten, T. M. and Whittle, S. (2004) 'TransPanthers: The greying of transgender and the law', *Deakin Law Review*, Vol. 4, No. 2, pp. 503–22

Woodward, K. (2008) 'Gendered bodies, gendered lives', in Richardson, D. and Robinson, V. (2008) *Introducing Gender and Women's Studies*, Basingstoke/New York, NY: Palgrave

Zhou, J. N., Hofman M. A., Gooren L. J. and Swaab D. F. (1995) 'A sex difference in the human brain and its relation to transsexuality', *Nature*, Vol. 378, No. 6552, pp. 68–70

INDEX

Note: page numbers in *italics* denote tables or figures.